Pearls of
Wisdom

פנינה בינה

WRITE TOGETHER™ PUBLISHING

Nashville, Tennessee

Published by Write Together Publishing™ LLC.
www.writetogether.com

ISBN 1-930142-59-5 Paperback
ISBN 1-930142-66-8 Hardback

Title: Pearls of Wisdom. Subject: 21st century literary collections.
(Multiple authors).

For Write Together Publishing:

Publisher: Paul Clere

Editor: John D. Bauman

Cover & Book Design: Bill Perkins

To publish a book for your school or non-profit organization that comple-
ments your academic goals or values, vision and mission, please contact:

WRITE TOGETHER™ PUBLISHING
533 Inwood Dr.
Nashville, TN 37211

phone: 615-781-1518
fax: 520-223-4850

www.writetogether.com

Pearls of Wisdom

פנינה בינה

by the Students
and Faculty of
The Marsha Stern Talmudical Academy
Yeshiva University School for Boys

Pearls of Wisdom

Staff

Editors-in-Chief	Phil Bomzer
	Judah Rothstein
Assistant Editor-in-Chief	Simmy Siegel
Director of Submissions	Jeffrey Kilstein
Assistant Director of Submissions	Zevy Hamburger
Director of Advertising/Events Coordinator	Zohar Kastner
Fundraising	Max Wein
	Zohar Kastner
	Simmy Siegel
Editors and Layout Editors	Eli Hamburger
	Avi Katz
	Zohar Kastner
	Shaul Lifshitz
	Eliot Orenstein
	Simon Papiashivili
	Shimon Rosenbaum
	Brian Waxman
Artists	Shaul Lifshitz
	Max Wein
Principal	Mr. Ya'acov Sklar
Dean	Rabbi Dr. Michael Hecht
Faculty Advisor/Coordinator	Ms. Sandra Schamroth

Table of Contents

Faculty Works

Foreword

It is essential that students are deeply involved in writing, that they share their texts with others, and that they perceive themselves as authors. I believe these three aspects are interconnected. A sense of authorship comes from the struggle to put something big and vital into print and from seeing one's own printed words reach the hearts and minds of others.

The students who submitted original works to this year's *P'ninei Binah, Pearls of Wisdom,* produced quality, creative work. It is obvious that our students, under the supervision of Ms. Schamroth, spent endless hours writing and editing the material enclosed in this book, and I congratulate them. As educators, we find it essential to provide our students opportunities to study and write, time to pursue their own important projects, mentors who inspire, and chances to work collaboratively.

I am immensely proud of the students' achievement, and I am confident that their dedication and love for writing will continue.

Mr. Ya'acov Sklar
Principal

Note from the Editors

The words *P'ninei Binah* are Hebrew for *Pearls of Wisdom*. This title has a double meaning. It is an expression of how we truly feel about our students' creative and literary skills as well as a memoriam of a former English teacher, Mrs. Pearl Mayefsky. This publication is a tribute to her care for and dedication to her students. We would like to thank the Marsha Stern Talmudical Academy as well as our sponsors for helping to fund this special edition. We would also like to give a special thank you to Ms. Sandra Schamroth who put this idea into motion. And we would especially like to thank the students who have made this publication a reality.

Phil Bomzer and Judah Rothstein
Editors-in-Chief

About Our School

The Marsha Stern Talmudical Academy/Yeshiva University High School for Boys is dedicated to synthesizing a rigorous Torah education with a superior general studies program. We emulate Yeshiva University's Torah Umadda philosophy, uniting secular and religious studies to provide a way of life and purpose for every student. We encourage students to explore academic areas, develop relationships with other students and their teachers, and make the four years they spend at our school a time of thinking, feeling, and doing. After their time in our yeshiva, the overwhelming majority of our students learn in Eretz Yisrael, go on to college and graduate school, and then assume leadership positions in their communities.

Pearls of Wisdom

The
Students of

The Marsha Stern Talmudical Academy
Yeshiva University High School for Boys

פנינה בינה

Prometheus Unchained

Michael Rosman
Grade 12

As I flex my spiritual muscles
I reach toward the sky
My soul vigorously hustles
As again and again, I try

For fifteen years
I've been working out
With my laughter, with my tears
Desiring belief, filled with doubt

Resisting temptation
Ignoring derision
Send me your salvation
Guide me to the right decision

I avoid each mocking smile
Every taunting word
I walk the extra mile
Where no sound is heard

My friends have broken rank
Have joined the swelling revolution
They roll on like an enemy tank
Filling the air with stench of its pollution

Where are my comrades of yesterday
When we shared a bench together
They have all left me, I fear
They have all wandered far, far away

I must ignite the flame
From the dying fire
I must eradicate the shame
Wash away the mud and mire

From the smoldering embers
The phoenix will again arise
Fear not the hell-bent horde's members
To the brave and righteous will go the prize

Each day will bring me closer to my goal
Each day my lost ones will be regained
Helping each other out of the deep black hole
Prometheus unchained

Gum
Michael Bernstein
Grade 9

Squashed on a sidewalk,
Lying there.
Sad,
Silent.

Imprinted with someone's shoe pattern,
Lonely.
Its pink majesty lost,
Gray.

Open another pack.
But this time, cherish
Your gum.

Roadysseus
Michael Gordon
Grade 11

As constant as the sun, he arrives every morning in his majestic golden vehicle, and again every evening lined up in a caravan with his compatriots. He is the bus driver, the Colossus of Roads, the brave and hearty soul who fearlessly ferries passengers from point A to point B. Read his story, know his adventures and tip accordingly.

At the earliest signs of morning, the bold bus driver heads off on his journey. He is a gladiator of the coliseum known as the highway. He challenges the elements that try to hinder him from his mission of transportation. He sets out on the road while many still lie sleeping in their beds, and like Hyperion, the son of Apollo the Sun god, mounts his glowing chariot and awakens the world with his mighty horn. Once he has banished sleep from all the houses he passes, the bus driver rides on to pick up his passengers and take them to their destination.

At each stop the bus driver honks and waits, sometimes improvising by waiting then honking, or honking repeatedly until someone opens the door. Many on his route avoid any confrontation with him, for he is like Charon, the boatman of Hades, who brings the dead to their miserable doom. So it is with the bus driver: at each stop corpse-like individuals clamber on board and sit, mute and deaf to the world. If no one answers his honking, the bus driver must use his keen sense of judgment to decide how to proceed. His training serves him well. In the final seconds before he departs the premises, the bus driver puts all his strength into pushing on the horn, sending one last honk that wakes the walking dead.

Along his trek the bus driver may encounter numerous other perils which test his wit and mettle. Roads may be blocked by the foul smelling giants that roam the streets devouring all the refuse in their paths. In such cases the courageous bus driver must maintain the discipline of patience, easing his way past the massive beast and enduring the rank odor emanating from its hindquarters. Angry motorists may attempt to confound his senses with their incessant beeping and swearing, or frustrate his voyage by cutting in front of his vehicle. But, being an experienced denizen of the bustling streets, our hero knows the digital dialect with which to deal with such rage-filled commuters. With a simple, yet well practiced, hand motion the bus driver deftly expresses his view of the situation and clearly explains that the other drivers will have to wait their turn. On occasion, the mighty bus driver may well hear the wailing of the siren's song. In such instances he must steal himself away from the temptation to follow the source of the blaring sound and gaze upon whatever horrible accident summoned it. After escaping from paying the toll trolls, the daring bus driver may find himself fleeing from the howling blue and white banshees, the scourge of the road. The bus driver must then make another choice, to floor it or to pull over...

Will our hero escape unharmed? Will he get his passengers to their destination on time? Will he be serving five to ten years for resisting arrest and endangering the lives of minors? To find out, please send ten drachma to Homer, PO Box 978, Athens Greece or go online to TheBlindBard.com (credit cards are accepted).

Thoughts from Above

Chaim Feigenbaum
Grade 11

I don't get it.
Why don't they see
All the pain
They are causing me?

Where did they go wrong?
What was the cause?
Why can't they recognize
Their many many flaws?

It's not so difficult;
All you need is a little heart
If everyone in the world
Would just play his part.

You will have no more worries,
I will erase all your fears,
No more pain and prosecution
I will dry up all your tears.

I am waiting for them to come home
Then I will return
To the promise land of Israel
When will they learn?

But I won't give up on you, my children.
I know you will find your way.
When we all join hands as one people
Oh, what a glorious day.

Atlantis
Yaakov Strauss
Grade 10

Once upon a time,
By a city on the sea,
There was a certain chime,
For the city was not to be.

It was a magnificent place,
With many people up and abound,
However they would soon not take up space,
For soon not even the island would be around.

Atlantis was the city's name;
It was very advanced indeed,
Life to the people was not a game,
To be honest and learned was their creed.

The people knew many things
And had knowledge beyond their years,
And it was because of greedy kings
That their faces would be full of tears.

The king's greed knew no bounds,
And all he cared for was gold;
The gold was found in the grounds,
Under the island on which this story is told.

The king dug up all the ground
In order to get his gold.
As a result there were floods abound,
Of which no one was told.

And then it happened one fateful day
That the sea engulfed that great place.
Because of greed did the great people pay,
And nothing remained, not enlightenment nor grace.

Never was there a city such as this,
Nor never again will there be
A city filled with so much bliss
That was swallowed by the sea.

Broken Light

Jonathan D. Stettin
Grade 9

It was after me again
Constantly chasing me
Always lurking
Relentless pursuit
         Yet I remained ahead
Running and hiding
Anything to get away
Just keep going
Never stop
         I have always been ahead
Ghastly silence
Must have stopped
Rest, relax, rethink
Haunting resumed
         I must get ahead
It's catching up
It's right there
I can feel it bearing down
I can't keep this up
         No longer can I stay ahead
I've lost
I know it
I must confront it
I turn around
         No longer am I ahead
I face it
It stops, briefly
It flashes brilliantly
It consumes me
         No one is ahead
White, bright, light-blinding
It enters into me
My body and mind are wracked
I remember
         I am hurled behind

It finally caught up
I've been running for so long
I thought I could escape
But my past wouldn't be avoided
         I am far behind

Nothing is the same
My present is ruined
My future is shattered
I begin again
    I am where I started, long ago
I'm trying to rebuild
I must salvage
Chances are slim
I must try
    I will be where I was
It's been a struggle
Many painful years
I couldn't let it defeat me
It didn't defeat me
    I *am* again

An Unexpected Seder in Baltimore

Nechemia Aronoff
Grade 11

It was early Sunday morning when the Brown family (a modern orthodox Jewish family) left from Lawrence, NY, to go to Florida in their Dodge Ram for *Pesach.* They thought that they would make it there by late Monday afternoon at about six o'clock with making pit stops for saying prayers, using the bathroom, and eating meals. The first Seder was scheduled on Wednesday night. Unfortunately, the Browns did not leave time for the early spring snowstorm that wiped out the whole upper East Coast. By the time they reached the Baltimore exit on I-95, three and a half inches of snow had accumulated on the ground. The Browns, knowing that Baltimore is a nice Jewish community, got off the highway and went to Yeshivas Ner Israel, the well-known yeshiva in Baltimore. They stayed in a motel near Pikesville for the night until it stopped snowing. By the morning, the snow increased in intensity. It was snowing harder and thicker than it had ever snowed before.

Mrs. Brown said to her husband Bill, "Should we risk driving down to Florida, or should we stay here?"

Bill answered his wife Jill, "The roads are hazardous, and driving is dangerous. But I really think that sharing the Seder with a Rabbi from the Yeshiva will be a nice experience for the family." Jill agreed with him, and they told the children Avi, Malkie, David, and Shanie, about their decision to stay in Baltimore for the Seders.

David said to Avi, "This stinks. All of our friends took planes down to Florida and are in the hotel now, but we get stuck here, in Baltimore, with a bunch of 'Black Hat Rabbis.'" Avi, the oldest child in the family, tried to calm David down while trying to see the good points of their seemingly bad situation.

Bill called up the Yeshiva and asked for the phone numbers of some of the Rabbis who taught at the Yeshiva. He spoke to the secretary. "Our family is now stranded in Baltimore en route to Florida for *Pesach*. We have no family or friends in the area and are hoping to be able to spend the first days of *Pesach* with one of the Rabbis and his family." The secretary informed Bill that the Yeshiva had a list of available hosts for the holiday and proceeded to give him a few names.

Bill called up Rabbi Horowitz and explained the situation. "Rabbi," he said, "We are in a difficult situation." Rabbi Horowitz told Bill that he and his family would be very happy to host the Brown family for *Pesach*. Luckily, the Rabbi also had several children. Some of them were the same ages as the four Brown children. The children would share rooms with his children. The parents could sleep in the guest room.

The Browns enjoyed the Seder at the Horowitz's home. They had such a good time that the children begged their parents to spend the rest of *Pesach* in Baltimore. Now a new tradition has been established for the Brown family. Instead of going to Florida every year for *Pesach*, they now go to Baltimore to be with the Horowitz family.

Avi summed it up best. "We really did have a fun time. Rabbi Horowitz is pretty cool, even if he does wear a black hat. His children were really lot of fun, and on *Chol HaMoed*, they showed me how to make really neat Hebrew signs on the computer. I really want to go back again next year."

In the Coliseum
David Krup
Grade 11

Down in the house of play
      rain out of the sky
I was in the back
      While you were?
I still don't know why
Then you were gone, gone, gone,
I was alone again,
Which leads to green trouble
The rain no longer by itself,

         I felt abandoned
I left the house of play
         And went for a wet-walk,
             To never forget
They said I'd be okay, but I'm not sure I'll be
         I felt abandoned
         Now it's salty, eternally branded paintings shrieking of green
It haunts me to be abandoned,

Still it haunts me, like a wall with no end

Three Old Men at Separate Tables

Elyada Goldwicht
Grade 9

I am
one of them
how did we get here?
What happened to
our lives and years?

This appears to be a calm Sunday
evening.
The waiters move among us.
We are poured water, coffee and wine
while awaiting our order.

Where have the wars gone?
Where have even the tiny agonies
gone?
This place has found us.
The white table cloth and the shiny utensils,
glimmer for our fingers

Such calm is ungodly but
fair.
For, in a moment, we remember the
hard years and those to come.
Nothing is forgotten; it is merrily put
aside.
Like a glove, a gun,
a nightmare

Subway

Joel I. Ryzowy
Grade 10

The meaning of the phrase "beauty is in the eyes of the beholder" really stands out when analyzing the beauty of the New York subway system. To some people the subway system, including the cars and the stations, are really disgusting. But to me, New York City's "underground" is a beautiful historical asset.

The 181st street station on the "A line" is, to many, truly an ugly station. You enter the station through the ugliest doors, painted in a dark, seaweed color. You pass the doors, but they screech, yelling back at you for opening them. You proceed down the ramp, which is black as burned toast. The tiles, which were once white, are now the color of an elephant's skin. As you continue going down, you enter an unpleasant botanical garden blooming with mildew on all sides.

Finally after a long hallway of distinctly opaque colors, you reach the turnstiles. However, before entering, you must pass the clerk. It is not enough that the clerk does not even smile at you, but no one makes eye contact with the clerk. You reach out for your "Gold Metrocard" and swipe it at the turnstile. "Try Again" reads the display. After the tenth "Try Again," you receive a "GO." As you cross the turnstile, you hear the noise of the rusty rails, signifying that the train is coming. However, you cannot even get to the stairs because of the large crowd of fellow commuters pushing you left and right. As you approach the stairs, you hear the painful sound, "Stand clear of the closing doors." Now you know that you must waste another twelve minutes for the next arriving "A train." As you stand behind the yellow line, the smell of urine and garbage is overwhelming. While smelling this concoction, you see rats running on the tracks. Finally, the train arrives, and you hope to get a seat. The worst thing that can happen to you now is that, after a long day of work or school, you would have to transfer to a different train and go through a similar, painful process all over again. No wonder the New York City subway has such a bad reputation when compared to other metro lines. After going through this everyday, people become stressed and annoyed.

However, to me, the subway represents history. The New York City subway made the first steps to a safe and inexpensive commute. Its creation was the first of its kind. In the subway, both old and modern worlds meet. You enter the station with probably the same doors that were placed there a century ago. The beautiful mosaic arrangement of the tiles gives some stations an antique look. You walk down a long ramp that leads to your destination. You reach the turnstiles, the gateway to the city. The electronic turnstiles give it a modern "taste." You walk down stairs coated with generations of colors of paint and wait for the next arriving "A train." As you wait for your train, you experience New York—underground. A melting pot of cultures is presented to you. People with all types of problems mix in an ethnic environment located only in the New York subway system.

The train finally arrives. As you are seated in the bucket seats parallel to the window, you see New York's assets. While crossing the hundred-year-old Manhattan Bridge, your view is that of other New York landmarks. The Brooklyn Bridge stands firm over the water, and the Statue of Liberty salutes you as you pass.

The subway's service is unbelievably reliable and fast. The system can take you anywhere in the city at an affordable price. I personally enjoy the subway because of its speed and efficiency. The subway is one of New York City's biggest assets because it takes people like me where I want to go.

Beauty is in fact in the eyes of the beholder. To many, the subway is a very stressful experience because of all the hustle that must be encountered to finally get to their destination. However, within the historic tunnels of the New York City subway, the various "walks of life" and differing perspectives come together for a common productive goal.

The Tempest
Simeon Siegel
Grade 11

A dark ominous wind clouded the sky
It left humankind an aura of fear and hate
The harbinger of anger camouflaged the night
And swallowed up all sense of virtue and light.

Then the rain came thrashing down
With it came the flash of light
Then roared the boisterous thunder
And then surfaced the deadly twister.

Tearing up everything in sight
Leaving a path of devastation
Not allowing a sole survivor
To live to tell its tale of danger.

And then just as it seemed to cease
And bring back life to the barren land
The endless storm regained its might
And threatened the world with eternal plight.

And then abruptly the skies cleared
It left its mark upon the world:
The path of devastation crowding the earth
And made way for the rainbow's birth.

The Best Advice I've Ever Received
Philip Bomzer
Grade 12

Good advice is hard to come by, so when some comes along it's a good idea to take it. During my lifetime I have gotten some really good advice such as "Watch your mouth," "Don't go swimming until one hour after you eat," and "Don't touch that! You don't know where it's been." My own personal bit of advice to all of my friends is "Don't jump in front of moving cars." Most of them dismiss it with an "I know that," or a "Moo," and that's just fine with me. I don't like them that much anyway. All I know is that I listen to advice when it's given, and it's given quite often. People are always telling me to "Go jump in a lake," "Take a long walk off a short pier," or "Get out of my face." I'm always thankful when someone is nice enough to take some time out of his own life in order to correct something drastically wrong in mine.

As I said, I've been given some great advice during my years on this planet, but the best advice I've ever received came from a very unexpected source. It was during my elementary school years, when I was known as "Shut Up." One hot winter's day, as I sat at my desk building architectural marvels out of Lego blocks, a fellow classmate approached me with an intriguing proposition: if I would convey him one of my Legos he would be obliged to give me one of his palate pleasing confections. I couldn't believe the words that had just escaped my peer's lips. Did he really have the audacity to ask me to compromise my artistic freedom by destroying a work of art just for a meager cookie?! I was still angry minutes later as I devoured the last piece of my tainted pastry. My early morning surrender hung over me like a storm cloud for the rest of the day. My naptime was not as restful, the stories had no happy endings, the glue was not as tasty, the caviar was rotten, and the champagne was only room temperature.

As I dragged myself up the stairs from the lunchroom, I came to the realization that the only solution was to confront him that afternoon. So while all the others were enjoying their pudding cups, I casually strode across the room to where my nemesis manifested himself. As I got closer and closer my nerves began to tense. I was never more afraid in my entire life. My thoughts began to wander: what would I say? what would I do? how many chucks could a woodchuck chuck if a woodchuck could chuck wood? Before I knew it, I was face-to-face with my adversary. Since I hadn't thought this far ahead, I did the only thing I could think of. I grabbed the Lego and ran. I ran like the wind, past the blocks, around the stuffed animals, through the playhouse. I ran so fast that I didn't have enough time to stop before running into the teacher who was accompanied by my rival, now crying uncontrollably. The teacher picked me up and brought me to the other side of the room where she gave me the best advice I have ever received in all of my years: "Stand in the corner and don't turn around until you've thought about what you've done and learned your lesson."

Her words hit me like a ton of bricks. This "corner" she spoke of was obviously a metaphor for our minds; the lesson: our purpose for being.

That day I stood in the corner, tall and proud, and haven't turned around since.

Free Your Mind

Asher Fredman
Grade 12

Somewhere upon the hills of York
Or the bank of Thames
Or a crescending icy peak
Majestic without name
Stood a formless creature
Who may have once been a man
But who had so morphed into a stage
Unseen since life began
But this unnatural figure
Withered, immeasurably aged
Knew more than the brilliant scholar
Or the wisest sage
He had more strength than a king
Or the greatest feudal lord
The fury that he could unleash
Outdid the Mongol hordes
On the great mysteries of life
If asked he could expound
Explicate to man's limited mind
He could unnerve and astound
To him the Bard's greatest verse
Was but child's speech
His philosophies were so advanced
As beyond Socrates' reach
This man was one of the first
The 23rd to be exact
To inhabit the new earth
Adam's cousin in fact
But he had left the fruitless pursuit
Of Eden reentry
Agriculture held no appeal
Nor primitive industry
Instead, this man like none before
Wandered the virgin earth
Following his meandering mind
Across its breadth and girth
He was the first to contemplate
Those questions which
Continue 'til this day and on
To men's minds, bewitch

Once he started walking
He just walked on and on
Acquiring knowledge on his way
His mind drifted beyond
The self-imposed constraints we use
To keep our world sane
The questions we will not discuss
Answers we won't explain
Through thousands of years he has continued
From civilization no request
Satisfied with his mission
On life's never-ending quest
He keeps his mind free and pure
For now, that is his choice
He is just waiting for a world ready,
Willing to hear his voice

Time

Chaim Feigenbaum and Jonathan Lauer
Grade 11

A man stands in the doorway
I walk over to him, and I say "hey"
He responds with a grin and then a smile
Then we depart to run—my ultimate trial.

My boot: it covers my delicate feet
So I can prepare for life's track meet.

But this is no normal meet that I will run in
It is the race against time, which I hope to win
Time is the man who stands in the doorway
And I hope he never catches up to me on any given day.

Untitled
Avi Katz
Grade 12

When people hear all these sayings about life, "Don't let it pass you by," "Take advantage of it before it takes advantage of you" and so on and so forth, does it really hit home what these terms mean? To tell you the truth, I didn't and probably still don't believe and understand when people say these things.

As a teenager growing up in a morally corrupt and hostile world, I am every day more and more coming to the realization, which people do not often enough try to make abundantly clear, that this society we live in has teeth and will not be afraid to use them. We might be wearing our name-brand shirts and our $150 sneakers, but it won't always be like that.

The opportunities given to us in our youths should never be taken for granted like they have been so many times over and over again. While we should never lose our childhood, we have a responsibility to ourselves to look farther than what's in front of our faces. If we don't take this privilege to heart, if we start abusing what was so graciously given, then those teeth marks shall forever remain scarring each one of us for life, no matter what the outcome becomes.

Commando
Natan Zohar
Grade 10

A commando there was, one of the nation's best
Who protected the country. Cover ops were his forte
A brave man to go undercover with the rest
Of his troop. His arsenal was mighty;
Weapons of every type were in his possession
And he used them to let out his pent-up aggression.
Slung over his shoulder was an AK-47
Which sent many a foe to heaven.
He even had a two and a half foot scythe.
In his boot was a survival knife
That had a blade of stainless steel
And caused several wounds that could never heal.
Strapped across his body were two belts of ammo
That made him look like a psychotic Rambo.

A Very Special Person

Hillel Weingarten
Grade 11

My name is David, and I am almost eleven years old. I write this because what I am about to tell you is very important, not just for you, but also for everyone in this world. I have a very close relative who is mentally retarded.

Unfortunately, when such a child is born, he needs much caring, much more than any other child. It's very hard for one to deal with such a family; the other siblings don't get half the attention as the special child. In addition, there are many costs included in the teaching and/or medical care needed. Then there's the greatest cost of all: the love, care, and time the parents show specifically for the child.

Besides the fact that the other siblings in the family don't get enough attention, there are other difficulties that arise. For example, there are some people who don't want to be friends with me because my relative is mentally retarded. They say behind my back, "Oh my gosh, I can't go over to his house. His relative is retarded, how does he deal with it?" People don't know how much this hurts me; they really think that it's contagious or something. I used to think, "Why do I have to have a retarded child in my family; he does me no good. I have no friends because of him. My parents don't seem to think that I am alive. Why do I have to have this?" In my prayers I used to ask G-d, "Why did you have to give my family a special kid?" Then I realized how wrong I was.

Many people either put down retarded children or think that they can't talk to the kids because they are "messed up." This is totally false! These special children do have brains and can understand what you say! They have feelings.

One must realize that G-d only gives these special children to special people. There are only some people who can deal with such a difficulty. No it's not a burden; it's almost like a blessing. These children are special, and no one should dare put them or a family member down in any way.

Once I heard my friend say, "Are you retarded or something?" No one can imagine how I felt at that instant. It felt like my life had stopped for a few seconds. These people don't understand how painful that "joking" phrase is. My purpose in writing this is, hopefully, understood. If not, please, whoever you are, before you say or think something negative about someone who has an illness, just think how that person feels; put yourself in his situation. Then, you can talk and think about such a situation. Thank you all for taking just a few minutes to read my request.

A Tribute to Rabbi Dulitz
Jason Scharf
Grade 10

In New Orleans,
In the nineteen thirties,
Little Label was born
Near a golden field of corn.
The boy soon became a young man,
And higher education at Y.U. was the plan.
To study under the beloved Rov
With dedication, purpose, and love.
Smicha was the next rung on the ladder
What he learned obviously mattered.
A teacher at M.T.A. he became
That is his claim to fame.
Turning pages in the air,
His words spewing without a care.
No doubt he's got a brilliant mind;
He's truly one of a kind!

Hero
David Krup
Grade 11

Remember when the hero was a good guy
Fallen from grace what a disgrace
Ol' faithful no longer dependable. He reflects us
There's no wood in the fireplace and no one seems to care
Potential in the sky but he's afraid to fly
We've fallen from grace what a disgrace
What has happened to us?
Where did it all go
When did it all go
He's afraid to fly.

Gatsby Vs. Superman

Simmy Siegel
Grade 11

In F. Scott Fitzgerald's novel *The Great Gatsby,* many hidden themes are presented to the reader. From the first sentence to the last we are thrust into a world of veiled implications in which we can view the actions of different individuals. The last paragraph of the narrative centers on one main theme that has pervaded the story. It adheres to the idea that Gatsby believed in his power to repeat the past and to change it as he saw fit. He thought he could regain the affection of Daisy, his long lost love, but failed and was killed in the effort. As it says in the tale, he believed in "the green light." This green light symbolizes many different ideas. In Shakespearean classics, it was one of the four humors, bile. Traditionally, it has come to represent money, jealousy, and success. All of these can apply to Gatsby's character, as well as to the themes of the book.

However, I would like to take a different approach. I believe that the green light is a strong allusion to the "Man of Steel." The "Man of Steel," a.k.a. "Superman," was propelled from his native planet seconds before its explosion. He was launched to Earth and adopted by a young couple that raised him as their own. However, understanding that he didn't fit in, Superman longed to repeat and change the past. For this reason he searched for a way to overcome the bounds of time and remedy his situation. He believed that this could be achieved if he had something from his homeland to work with. With this in mind, he turned to the bright green stone of his planet, known formally as "Kryptonite." He believed that this green gem would help him to mend the present. He believed that this green light held all of the answers and when he found it, he was elated.

This is parallel to the case of *The Great Gatsby.* Although not endowed with prodigious potential, Gatsby sought to acquire the love of Daisy that he had lost in the past. For this reason he bought a house in West Egg. And when he discovered the green light, he too was elated. Both had found their solution in this shining green light. But that was only when viewed from afar. For when Superman approached the pebble, he discovered its deadly effect. When Gatsby neared the green light, he found that, to his dismay, he had lost Daisy forever. The green light's sparkle had deceived both men. And both men were dissatisfied with the turnout. Gatsby still believed that Daisy would come running to him, and Superman ended up discovering that he could go back in time by spinning around the world backwards several times. Through both of these characters, we are shown that even supermen are people and as such have weaknesses that need to be remedied.

From a Different Perspective

Shaul Lifshitz
Grade 11

They came to my home and burst through my doors
And put me in shackles and chains
I was lost in confusion, threw a glance at my wife
And my children, whose fate was the same.
There were shouts all around us, in the house, in the yard,
And tears were flowing from my eyes.
We were led to a wagon by our merciless captors;
I thought that for sure I would die
The shock had resided, and my mind became clear
And I thought about what I had done
Nothing, not one—I was an innocent man.
Yet, I was captured and watched with a gun.
Now I envisioned my end, and I knew it was near.
Through my body, chills coldly did sweep
I hunched up in the corner, bent my head to my knees
And started to openly weep.
My weeping turned into wailing and my wailing into screaming
I kicked my legs like a child
When I was bashed on the head by my adversary's gun
All went black. I was out for a while.
When I awoke it was dark; I barely could breathe.
I was cramped in a damp wooden room
With hundreds of others in the same situation.
I went back to my sleep, to my doom.
I awoke again later, in the same dampened room
And a new sudden fear swept through me
With hundreds around, I was still all alone
Without my own dear family.
I couldn't search for them, we all looked the same
All gloomy and tired and weak;
All men, women, children, all ages and sizes
With futures that seemed quite bleak.
I sat in my space, and the room started rocking
To and fro as waves carried us forth
With the air getting colder, the sea getting rougher
I guessed we were headed north.
After months upon months of traveling like this
Scrunched up day in and day out
We came to a stop, and our captains above deck
Began to give orders and shout.

A kick opened the door and let in the light
And I saw a horrible sight.
Of the hundreds of hundreds that started this journey
Two thirds of them had died,
Our shackles still tight, our chains still tied.

Off the ship we were led like cattle
Like a circus procession with lions and clowns
And riders standing up on their saddles.
We were put in more wagons; there I met my wife
And my children; the youngest had died.
I went back to my corner and with my wife and my kids
Together we all sat and cried.
We were sent to a chamber to be showered and cleaned
I was separated from my family
Then led up to a stage in front of a crowd.
Of my family I never did see.

There was bidding and yelling and waving and shouting
A man came onto the stage
Looked me over and said, "He is healthy. He's strong.
He's fit. He will do. I will pay."
A transaction was made, and he took me away
To his house high up on a hill.
He gave me some food, some shelter, and some clothes,
But he took from me my free will.
There I met others like me, who had families,
But, like me, they were taken away
And they were sold into hands which made them slaves.

Now, twenty years later, I think of my home
Myself, my wife, and my children
All taken by force, as if we were objects, not people,
All because of the color of my skin.

Another Day
Yaakov Meir Nemoy
Grade 11

It was another gray afternoon in the middle of December. Naturally the New York air was tearing between the buildings and trying to bite my ears off with its sheer strength. Everywhere around me people were going about their business, grumbling as usual. The gloominess of the day only made them grumble more. At least that's what I think, but no one remembers, anymore, any clear days when people grumbled less. Some people think after the atomic leak in New Palestine, the weather was permanently changed. Others say that all of the electrical interference from cell phones created the clouds and occasional lightning storms. All I know is that we messed things up.

I stepped into a small bagel shop to buy lunch, and there was a long line. Everywhere around me people were pushing and shoving to make the line move faster. I tried my best not to get pushed out of the line, but everyone around me seemed to be obsessed with getting his food before me. After I bought my food, I decided to eat in my room. I didn't want to go through the whole pushing game to get a seat somewhere.

When I got to my room, my roommate was there surrounded by yet another new computerized object. He looked up at me and pointed out his new game cube along with all of the games he got. I looked at them, and I noticed all of these games involved killing someone. I looked through his CD case, and I saw that in the back of the case there was a game called "Escape from Fairyland." I asked him what it was, and he said that it was just a game he got for his little brother, but it was still a decent game.

I popped the CD in his machine to take a look at it. I started playing the game, and I saw that I was holding an axe. I started to run around through a brightly lit forest, and I stopped in front of a fairy. I ran over to the fairy and started clicking on the axe to use it. The animated hand on the screen waved the axe around in the fairy's gut, and I watched as the fairy's stomach fell out. Another fairy ran up to my character, and I watched as the axe swung down and chopped the fairy in half. My roommate congratulated me when the game flashed that I got bonus points for artistic impression, but all I could think was, "Is this really a kid's game?" Right then I woke up.

Sometimes when we dream and our mind loses control, our body tries to tell us a message. At other times we can even see what might happen in the future. When I woke up I was trying to figure out which one it was.

The Bobover Tish

Ezra Rich
Grade 10

In Boro Park, a neighborhood in Brooklyn, N.Y., they live a holy life
With many children and a *tznius* wife.
On Friday night, after davening and a supper that was very sweet,
To 48th Street at 15th Avenue they went to meet
And eat the Rebbe's holy meat.
They went, knowing full well what to expect.
The Holy Rebbe, Rabbi Naftali Tzvi Halberstam Shlit''a
Would now eat his kugelah.
The Rebbe came out;
He had on a silver and gray cloak
And gave a stroke
To his long, gray beard.
He was now geared
To make the *Kiddush* to his Chassidim.
All of whom were *not* headed to *gehinom*
But rather on an express route to heaven.
The Rebbe ate and spoke
While waving from his long cloak.
The Rebbe ended his long meal,
Which did include some good veal.

Parents
Zohar Kastner
Grade 10

 In times of need and in times of greed your parents are there and your emotions are shared.

 When you're first born you cuddle in your mothers warm arms. She feeds you and nurses you until you can eat on your own. Every night you fall asleep to the lullabies of your mother's beautiful, sweet voice.

 After you fall in love with your mother, you are passed on to the love of your father. He teaches you to play baseball and, if you're lucky, even basketball. Eventually, he will teach you how to ride a bike and then how take a fight.

 After some years to come, your parents will sit you down and talk to you about drugs. After that talk they will bring on "the birds and the bees." You'll laugh and giggle until you burst but really this will help you in the years to come.

 So we see that your parents are the guides to your life, and they will point you in the correct direction. So listen to your parents and don't give them a fuss because your parents are the ones to trust.

The Middle Child
Yehuda Goldin
Grade 10

You are too young to stay up late
You are too old to fool around
You are too young so you must wait
You are too old to lie on the ground

You are too young to go outside and play
You are too old to play with toys
You are too young to drive away
You are too old to make a funny noise

You are too young to get a knife
You are too old to sing out loud
You are too young to have a wife
You are too old to draw a cloud

You are too young to go on a roller coaster
You are too old to go to school
You are too young to be on a poster
You are too old to swim in the kiddy pool

You are too young to go to work
You are too old to wear a diaper
You are too young to be a clerk
You are too old to be very hyper

You are too young to be home alone
You are too old to sleep late
You are too young to be fully-grown
You are too old to lose all that weight

You are the middle child

The Boxer
Daniel Douek
Grade 10

He is more powerful than any other.
He leaves his opponent crying for his mother.
His hair is in neat cornrows, eight in all,
And he weighs in at 215 pounds and is six feet tall.

They say his fists are made of steel,
But, I assure you, they are quite real.
He wears blue trunks with white stripes on either side.
He is a fair fighter; by all the rules does he abide.

I would never step into the ring with this beast
Because he would turn me into a Thanksgiving feast.

His skin is a very odd shade of brown;
In the ring he has never gone down.
While in the ring, he is not a nice fellow,
But outside I tell you he is rather mellow.

The Baker

Jeremy Erez
Grade 10

There once was a baker, a very friendly guy
None could pass his store and not stop in to buy.
He was a large man with quite a large belly
Probably from eating donuts filled with grape jelly.
His hair was white, both natural and from flour,
Which he covered with a hat that was as tall as a tower.
His shop was full of the pastries he liked to bake,
As well as pies, muffins, cookies, bread and cake.
He had a large family, his children numbered eight
And a wife who for forty years has been his mate.
They all worked together side by side, day and night
As they tried to make everything taste just right.
He baked for the townspeople and those who were royal
But no matter who his customer was, they all were loyal
For his food was delicious, the best in the land
And whatever he baked was always in demand.

The Policeman

Eliot Herman
Grade 10

Out there a policeman there was
Who did his best at whatever he does.
He loved coffee and doughnuts in the morning
Could not live without it or he would go in mourning
Very strongly built, he could make anyone into a bun
And his quest to make peace wasn't always much fun.
He fought the bad guys who did the crime
And made sure they did their time.
He had a police car that went very fast
To catch the criminals who had a bad past.
He had a badge and wore a uniform too
And used it to scare fugitives all the way to the "zoo."
Overall, he makes our society more exciting
By putting away the miscreants who make it unenticing.

The Bus Driver
Elie Kurtz
Grade 10

John was my old bus driver
And an incredibly lucky survivor
Of many big crashes and catastrophes,
At which he would only laugh, sneeze,
And continue, unscathed, on his way.
He would do his job every single day.
John would sit in his seat,
The students he would greet
As they walked onto the bus.
All about their teachers and schoolwork he would discuss.

Big John we would call him; he was quite old.
His beard was white, and his skin was a pale gold.
He loved his job with all his might
Even though he wasn't always treated right.
Sadly for John there wasn't much respect,
But if I wanted a friendly conversation, Big John I would surely elect.

Explorers
Steven Leybovich
Grade 10

There were *Explorers* among the bunch
Three or so fellows with their own hunch
Various lengths of broadness and bone
Each one of about sixteen stone
They were all curious on how things came about
Their curious natures were unique and stout;
Along they went on their undecided journey
Their logic surpassed superficial yearning
For each one had a skill of exploration they carried
As they journeyed through uncharted fields
Their exploration had produced great yields
They proved that through careful examination
Will come about great advances for a generation
Though these three or so would be thought of as naïve
When their initial concepts were conceived
As hackers they became perceived

Four Men

Michael Bernstein
Grade 9

Four men.
Four men in a room.
Four men in a room, isolated from the world.
Four men.

They were part of an experimental drug trial, specially treated to survive in a non-social atmosphere: Bob, Jim, Martin, and Carl. The drug was called SurVFit, named for "survival of the fittest," and it let them stay healthy, sane, and "normal" in a bare white room with no food, water, T.V., or other social contact.

But there were side effects.

You see, unbeknownst to the drug company, the formula of SurVFit had in it the chemical essence of primal competition. The months passed, and their attitudes grew increasingly hostile, then territorial, with each claiming a corner and staking it out. The only monkey wrench in the psychological works was boredom. They required no sleep and simply sat, guarding their corners, with no choice but to stay sane (the drug was still working).

And so, as always, the scientists fooled around in the lab, monitoring the four men through the cameras hidden in the room. These scientists were no different from any others and thought they were the smartest creatures G-d had ever placed on earth and didn't realize what a terrible thing they'd done. If you asked them, they couldn't be wrong, not in a million years!

And the months passed.

And the men, no longer really men, grew restless.

And the drug worked, and the scientists bragged, and the room stayed white.

And the months passed.

Finally, the scientists decided they had enough proof to market their "wonder drug." They went to check the cameras for the last time, but the cameras were smeared with something dark.

They opened the door and saw the terror they'd created.

There stood Martin in the middle of the room, towering over three bodies. And his grin was the grin of the devil, and his eyes burned with triumph, and he held three pairs of eyeglasses in his left hand.

And the demon spoke: "I got all the corners now."

And the scientists closed the door and decided not to sell their drug after all.

The Black Hole

Shaul Lifshitz
Grade 11

As I stare before me at the big black space
It seems to stare me back in the face.
I try, I try, but I can't comprehend
This big black thing; it doesn't end.
It captures my mind; it sucks me in.
I try to fight back; I know I won't win.
This black hole here, it's undefeatable.
If it takes you in, you're irretrievable.
But, alas, some hints, a tiny clue:
Small white markings coming through.
A foreign language, I don't understand,
Slowly but surely I raise my hand.
My name is called from somewhere beyond;
My heart is pounding like ducks on a pond.
Then, from somewhere inside me, my voice, soft and strained
Speaks up and asks, "Can you please explain?"
Then my teacher, yet again, goes through it once more
And I smile, 'cause I know I defeated the blackboard.

The Silence of Hate

Avi Katz
Grade 12

As they walked not knowing where they were going, they stared with
eager faces.
As they stood to be counted, they stared with eager faces.
As their clothing was taken from them, they stared with eager faces.
As they stood with all their pride taken from them, they stared with eager
faces.
As they stood with the last moments of life before them they did nothing
to protest, knowing they were staring with eager faces.
As we walked in the footsteps knowing where they had been, they stared
with hateful faces.
As we stood on the very ground that was once stained with our family's
blood, they stared with hateful faces.
As we stood in the exact place where the now mourned had spent their last
moment, we repeated the words that will forever silence those hateful
faces.
Never Again!

Who is the Free One?

Yoni Feiner
Grade 12

"For the first time you will see the truth," Keanu Reeves is told in the movie *The Matrix*. In a movie that describes how we live in a false world, Keanu Reeves's character Neo was required to go to a different environment in order to see the truth and realize that he was living a false life. So, too, in Bernard Malamud's novel *The Fixer,* the "fixer" Yakov Bok had to go to prison to discover the truth about what it means to be free and that freedom is in the mind, not the body.

In the opening segment of the novel, we are confronted with this man, Yakov Bok, who appears to have a horrible life. He was left as an orphan as a young child, he has always been poor, he wasn't able to have children, and his wife ran away with another man. It is not a surprise then that Bok, the fixer, would often curse G-d for the horrific life that has been bestowed upon him. The fixer thinks that, by leaving his shtetl (the small village where he lived), he would free himself of this life of misery and hopefully start anew.

As the novel continues, we find that, though Yakov was quite successful for a little while, his plans for a positive future were no longer possible, and he ended up in trouble. This was when Yakov began to mature. As he was being falsely accused, Yakov cried out, "My life is over because I've lost reason to live." It was at this point that Bok realized that life must have a purpose and that life is not merely about survival; rather, it is about doing something right. It was this philosophy that led Yakov to constantly refuse to sign and confess to the murder. Though he was tempted many times by officials saying that, if he admits that the Jewish people convinced him to murder the boy, he would go free, Yakov obstinately refused. Yakov began to realize that though physical freedom would save him a lot of pain, the pain of hurting others and going out of the prison an evil man is much worse. He felt that he could not admit to a lie and give in to them. Though in the past Yakov constantly cared solely about himself, we now see a new side of him; a man who is starting to learn that life is more than living—it's about doing the right thing.

In Jewish theology, there is a concept that, in order for a man to get a new start on life, he must cleanse himself of his sins of the past and, only then, is he considered like a new person. So, too, as part of Yakov's transformation into this more meaningful man, he was constantly regretting his previous actions. For example, the novel states, "Yakov reveried the past; the shtetl, the mistakes, and failures of his life." Furthermore, when discussing his feelings regarding Raisl, he notes that he should have treated her a little differently and been more conscientious of her needs. When he finally meets her, he says, "I've thought about our life from beginning to end and I can't blame you for more than I blame myself...Some people have to make the same mistake seven times before they know they've made it. That's my type and I'm sorry." By Yakov's recognition of his past faults, he was able to become a "new" person. He now realized that he had to act with more morality; as he noted, "Still I've suffered in this prison, and I'm not the same man I once was."

By the end of the novel, it becomes quite evident that Yakov has truly undergone a personal metamorphosis. One way the author highlights this is through his writing technique; the novel constantly goes back and forth between Bok's dreams and his reality. With this style, the author conveys to us the idea that Yakov found that his dreams, which symbolize one's perception, were often greater than reality, and that true freedom came through his mind, not his body. Bok realized that a man was not free unless he could act morally. It was through his experiences that Yakov saw the true light of freedom. "He was the experience. It also meant that now he was somebody else than he had been, who would have thought it?"

By going to this strange environment, Bok became a changed man. This past summer, I also went to a different environment that has enabled me to see things a little clearer and through a more enlightened lens. After visiting the concentration camps in Poland, where millions of Jews were slaughtered, I realized how fortunate I am not to have to live and die through what so many others had to suffer. Similar to Yakov Bok, one must be able to gain perspective and realize that life is about a greater purpose, and, only then, may we achieve true freedom.

The Dragon Slayer

Julius Strauss
Grade 11

My name is Ausarius, like that of my father and his before him. 'Tis this spirit which bore my own and the one that bore his spirit in turn that was the prelude to the honor of highest Dragon Slayer to King Arthur of England. Now this established title hath fallen upon my own head, with the death of my honored father. Though my experience lacks and though I have only but once seen a dragon, my heart is full, bounding with courage, and it knows no limit.

These past nights have been restless and rumor hath come to spread among the people of a dragon attacking villages on the east side of the Kingdom. Thus, with my sword passed down with age, my shield, and a word of praise and circumspection, I am off to vanquish the dragon. The nights, like the dragon, are long, cold and fierce, and to gaze at the night sky is to glimpse at the infiniteness of the dragon's scolding eyes. Still my heart is not lightened to my cause and I do pledge onwards, to a victory already foretold by the skill of my ancestors.

The ride has been long and arduous, and just as the night bears the glazing shine of the sun over its dark blanket, I have come to reach the easternmost village of the Kingdom. In this hour my eyes have come to see the indescribable landscape as the sun comes first to meet such a village in such a disastrous appeal, recently relieved of the nightly plague of the dragon. There is not much to see and all does appear without foundation, barren. It is a hard sight, for there are no souls and it does appear that I have missed the anguish of the people and the plight of the dragon. Now I must ride westward to the village whence I have just come. At best I will only meet its walls as the sun does set on the horizon. However, my cause is true and, if I must give my own life, I shall to protect the village of hundreds.

It does appear that fate has born reward to my effort, that I have come to reach the souls of the doomed village, still yet undoomed, an hour before the sun does release its protective hold upon us. The people are not without mind and they know of the dragon and its path; and though they are not easily nerved, they have come to face fate and listen to my tongue that does tell them to heed shelter as I do battle with the dragon.

The hour grows near, and the silence, the unwavering, blasting silence, a silence which by dawn may be the sweetest or most frightening sound that ever did meet the ear, now surrounds me. Yet I forge on with knowledge of my place in heaven, yet now not just so, for fate has dictated my victory, and it could not be that if I who am the best do lose, then the cause of the human will be left devastated by the being of a single monster born without kindness, wisdom, or heart, knowing only evil

Behold, the beast, the giant, the bringer of death, and the bearer of fire at its will, as it does move along the night sky, closer it grows...closer. Thrusting myself at it with my sword held out I hear it roar a blasting, deafening roar as it glides over me, and I feel the blood as it drips on my feet. However, as I gaze at the dragon still continuing towards the village, it does seem to be unscathed. Thus, the realization comes and looking back to my sword, I find it lying on the dust of the ground, next to my bloody arm. Then darkness overtakes me.

I awaken, not yet dead, and in the company of my saviors, whom I have not yet come to know by name. I am met with two unfamiliar feelings of dread and revenge. With the news of the entire destruction of yet another village and the greeting of the midday sun, I take foot and in more full-minded attempt plan a more noticeable attack against the dragon. Now the King who has come to know of the past two dragon rampages did send still seven of his best knights to join me against the dragon. Time has long since passed since the serenity of my dreams; and though I felt incapable of taking on the dragon, I stand here now, as the sun does once again fade, to engage the dragon, strengthened by the Knights.

Knowing the style of the dragon, we are prepared, and the attack unfolds. The dragon once again meets the sky, and a shrill not felt before entangles my spine. Glancing at the Knights I defeat my worries, and this time as the dragon glides down towards me it does not seem to ignore me quite as much as the last time. With a final breath I take foot in front of the dragon. Now the net does fly. In my mind the attack was great, the net swiftly throwing the dragon toward the ground, rendering the dragon prey to us. In my mind and not further. With this I feel myself being squeezed to death. Glaring back, I see myself being thrust from the dirt, as the net does cover only the head of the dragon. The net, useless, is ripped off the head of the dragon by its ferocious jaw and flung towards the ground. The dragon continues towards the village, and the sounds of the dead — my guilt no longer can bear it — scream in my ears. The heat of the dragon's breath blinds me; my mind does leave me and I know that my time has come and with this I jab my sword, the one I have clung to since first I took flight, into the belly of the beast. Once again the roar of the beast and the blood mingled in the unholiest of bonds as I do see that the horrifying sound of the beast is one against itself, and the blood, the happiest blood that ever did man see though engulfing me was not my own. The grasp is broken, and I fall to the ground. The descent is swift and it does come to me the picture of the lifelessness of my own self, quickly so. Still yet in a sight which did ever soothe my soul so, did I glimpse at the dragon and hear its last mighty roar as it met the earth with such strength that no life could surpass the impact of good or evil other than my own.

Partial Retrospective

Asher Fredman
Grade 12

On September 29, Ariel Sharon visited
property that technically belonged to the Israeli government,
and the Muslim Imams protested that the land was spiritually theirs.
Jews were outraged and claimed that the land had been given to their fore-
fathers
and they were the heirs.

The Palestinians say they have rights too, like the United Nation's Right of
Refugees
So both sides claimed to have legality, and the spiritual truth
And propaganda started, and riots, and stones, and fire, and guns, and hate.
It started in the street and rose and a kid got shot
And Joseph's tomb as hot with flames
And Ramallah with martyrs' names
In America people protested some, but mainly discussed
"Did you go to the rally? Yeah it was fun."

In the Arab nations people showed their anger, too
And emails, a deluge of emails until they became an end unto themselves
Showing strategically why that kid had to be shot
And people spoke, and speakers lectured, some had solutions others
refrained
The E.U. supported, the U.S. abstained
and leaders met and sipped cocktails
and ten-year-olds threw gravel, cocktails
and our leaders told us "they were never partners, they are ungrateful,
they use kids as shields and other inhumane practices"
and their leaders told them "look around, this is the Jews' fault, these
slums, they kill us mercilessly and engage in other inhumane practices"
and perhaps the killing will go on
Until everyone gets sick of it
Or until there aren't any kids left to throw stones or shoot rubber bullets
Or maybe one side will give up, and surrender to the other side's demands
Or maybe the earth will fall into the sun, the color of a mosque.

Eyes Shut
Simon Papiashvilli
Grade 11

Life is a palace,
I got lost in the forest in its backyard.

Love is a necklace,
I have the gold but no goldsmith in this country.

Life is a chalice,
For what I shall vainly look wide and far.

Beauty we see and we look away.
We see all but that we look astray.

The Best Advice I Ever Received
Uri Burger
Grade 12

When I arrived as a freshman, I was enthralled by the unlimited extra-curricular activities available at TMSTA. I attended many club meetings during my first few months, but I was most intrigued by the Business and Finance Club. The main function was participating in the New York State Stock Market Game, a game that gives students the opportunity to invest in the stock market online and follow their picks over a ten-week period. I had always paid attention to the stock market's fluctuations and always wished I could play the game myself without actually having to spend any money. I finally had my chance.

I didn't think I had the slightest shot of winning, but I wanted to play for the experience. I surfed the net and looked through the *Wall Street Journal* until I decided on the stocks I was going to buy. Because most of my picks were Internet-oriented, I felt fairly confident that I would at least make some money.

After the first week, I checked my rank. To my astonishment, not only was I in first place in my region, I was in first place in New York State. I started thinking of the possibilities. Could I really do it? Could I beat out over one thousand other teams and capture first place in a statewide competition? No, I thought. Besides, I'd never really won any competition before.

My sentiments were correct as I dropped to eighteenth place in the region the following week. However, as the ten-week competition progressed, I found myself moving closer and closer to the top spot. At the end of the eighth week, I was number one again. Slowly, my wildest dreams became reality. I was only two weeks away.

My portfolio continued to grow during the ninth week, and I assumed that I would still be in first place after Friday's close. However, when I saw my rank on Saturday night, my jaw dropped to the floor. I had dropped out of the top fifty and the first place team was almost $400,000 ahead of me. For a game that gives someone $100,000 to start out with and $100,000 to spend on margin, I thought there had to be a mistake. I figured that it was not possible to increase a portfolio by $500,000 overnight. But, I didn't question the integrity of the game. I figured I had come so far that I just couldn't stop there. The next day, Sunday, I cleaned out my entire portfolio and bought highly volatile stocks that could move thirty or forty points in a matter of days. I needed to make up a lot of ground in one week.

Monday night, I again went online to check the standings. I was in first place again! Since the rankings were updated weekly, I knew something had to be wrong. I checked my email and a letter from the coordinator of the region caught my eye. Apparently, there was a mistake in the system, which completely messed up the rankings. I was outraged. Had I done nothing, I still would have been in first place. However, because of the error, I was left with a shoddy portfolio and a huge feeling of disappointment. I told my father my problem. He said, "Uri, don't give up hope. If you deserve to win, then fight it. Never give up hope."

The next day, I spoke to the faculty advisor and told him my situation. He told me to call the coordinator of the region and see what to do. After leaving numerous messages on the woman's machine, I finally got through. I explained my problem to her and asked for her help. She gave me the telephone number of the Stock Market Game's offices, where the game is coordinated. I called them and told them the situation. At first, they were reluctant to do anything that would expose the mistake that they made. But, after persistent requests, they agreed that, if it were not for their computer error, my portfolio certainly would have been the top performer in the state. For the first time, there were two first place winners for the state.

The persistence has stayed with me throughout my four years at TMSTA. I eventually became President of the Business and Finance club as well as the Editor-in-Chief of the school newspaper. There are many times that I doubt whether I'll be able to accomplish an assigned task, but I never give up. With perseverance and hard work, I feel I can accomplish whatever I set my mind to.

Doubts
Simon Papiashvilli
Grade 12

As I look into the black holes,
And see the paper folds;

How will I ever get my share,
When I have never thought of fair?

Clocks fall from the sky;
Its arrows start to fly.

The arrows hit many hearts;
Most don't know these when not drawn on cards.

I found a treasure chest;
When is it going to be a fest?

My search has gone forever.
Eternity has gone forever.

Before and After
Etan Bednarsh
Grade 12

America is a nation that demands constant gratification. We can't wait in line; we need drive-thru windows. We need a news ticker at the bottom of the news and a sports report always right there for us to take, be it on television, the Internet, the radio, or, more recently, on a cellular phone or beeper. Without a doubt, speed is a crucial ingredient that makes up the American society.

In the election, however, more than speed, correctness must reign supreme. With the current uncertainty surrounding the presidential election, which has brought up so many issues, the nation must find out the true winner. Before we can discuss the validity of the Electoral College, we must reach a final decision on who won the Electoral College, as it is the system in place. It shouldn't matter how long the process takes as long as the correct choice comes out. The process should continue.

Many people are quick to point out all the shortcomings of our electoral process. I, however, feel that this prolonged recount is a microcosm of the beauty of America. When lesser countries might have collapsed under the pressure of this election, America has embraced the right to challenge and certify the voting process, and we have seen the importance of every American voice.

The election of 2000 has come to an end. Not a resolution, but an end. Rather than reaching the finishing point of this election maze, the process reached a screeching halt. The essence of reconciling the madness had to be deliberate to take as much time as necessary to reach the correct, true decision. In the end, the opposite occurred. The finality of the election occurred more from running out of time than from using the time they had to their advantage. This election was a disappointment for the United States, not because the wrong conclusion might have been reached, but because every action that could've been taken wasn't.

An Everlasting Superior

Samuel Damti
Grade 10

While ruminating over G-d's creations,
My soul is kindled by inspiration.
And wishing to make all people aware of his unique and miraculous supervision
Suddenly becomes one of my greatest ambitions.

If you ever feel your life is a mess,
Never give up; it all is but a test.
Things may seem like they're not going right,
But G-d has his reasons and knows what we like.

We were put in this world to serve one G-d;
He gave us each enough strength to withstand against all odds.
He gave us a body, a brain, and a soul,
And with them, he expects us to achieve his goal.

But we, G-d's nation, are often selfish and greedy;
We want everything for ourselves and give none to the needy.
And what we all sometimes forget is that G-d is our king,
And a king like G-d doesn't owe us a thing.

If you ever begin to do wrong,
Just remember to G-d you do belong.
You'll realize you should have never done that wrong deed,
And you'll repent and begin to look to life without any feelings of greed.

And sometimes our ego may swell,
And sometimes we neglect and rebel.
But we must remember, only with G-d we are safe,
And we are brought close to G-d only with faith.

We must remember the words of G-d and the words of the sages,
And we must realize we are merely specimens in cages.
So before your ego will soar, consider an eternal G-d is our king
And we are but a primitive being.

If not for G-d you would still be dust,
So take heed to G-d's words, for they are a must.
We are the people he chose from all nations,
So we owe him our thanks and deepest appreciations.

The Golem

Nechemia Aronoff
Grade 11

The Schwartzes, Herbert and Tillie, were an elderly middle-aged couple who lived in the old Jewish area of Los Angeles called Beverly Fairfax. At present, most of the Jews in LA have moved to the Valley or Beverly Hills, but back then, not long after World War II, most of the Jewish people lived there. The Schwartzes were discussing hiring a Japanese gardener for their little lawn. As they were discussing this important decision, in walked a very strange stranger.

The stranger walked stiffly, held himself stiffly, and talked stiffly. He also seemed weak on the social graces. He announced that he had something very important to say. Mrs. Schwartz was in the middle of presenting her opinion about hiring the Japanese gardener. Mrs. Schwartz was often in the middle of presenting her opinions on many topics. On these occasions, Herbert would often wonder why exactly he took early retirement.

Mrs. Schwartz did not relish being interrupted, especially by this strange stranger. "Herbert," she said. "Herbert, this fellow just walks in without a hello, or how-are-you, and makes announcements."

Herbert thought to himself, "How many times does Tillie do just that?" Of course he did not express himself out loud. "Now what is it you have to say? Maybe you would like some tea?" asked Herbert.

"I have much to say, and little time to say it" replied the stranger. "You should know that my arrival will mark a turning point for all mankind. It could be the end of the world as you know it."

The Schwartzes wondered what kind of a fellow just showed up. "Maybe he really needs some tea," Tillie said, looking at her husband. "What is his problem?"

The stranger stood up and was agitated. "You don't understand what I am," he said, more stiffly than before.

Herbert said, "What do you mean 'what I am'? Don't you mean 'who I am'?" He turned to Tillie and heard her say, "This one did not pass the immigrant's English class."

The stranger became more agitated. "I am not human," he shouted. "I am an experiment of the late Professor Styles at the nearby Cal Tech University. Professor Styles passed away, very recently and very naturally."

The Schwartzes knew all about the University. After all, their border Biff was a student at the community college. He was studying television.

"I bet you are in the same classes with our border Biff," proclaimed Tillie. "He is studying to be in television." The stranger seemed more upset than ever.

"I am trying to tell you that I am not human. I am the result of Professor Styles's experiments in cybernetics and robots."

The Schwartzes did not get it. "He really does need his tea" was Tillie's response.

"Our kind will be the end of the human," thundered the stranger.

Herbert jumped up. "Don't speak disrespectfully to my wife. Act properly!" yelled Herbert. He swung at the stranger. The stranger fell back, and lost his footing. He slipped and hit his head on the floor. It appeared that he was unconscious. Herbert looked at the stranger on the floor. Under his scalp the stranger had wires, springs, and other electrical parts. Herbert was clearly confused.

Then he said, "This creature does not seem to be human." He was less confused now. "You know that back in Prague (Herbert emigrated from Prague not too long ago) we had a Golem legend that was 400 years old. The Rabbi of Prague back then created a creature called the Golem. He made it live by writing the 4 letter name of G-d on its forehead." Tillie was not familiar with Golem legends.

"Well, does this have a holy name of G-d?" she asked.

Herbert examined the Golem. "No," he answered.

"Then why don't you put it there?" This was an order, not a suggestion.

"My grandfather in Prague was such a good scribe. He even taught me to write in the holy fashion," Herbert exclaimed. Herbert carefully inscribed the holy name on the Golem's forehead near the gash. He also fixed some wires that were exposed. As he worked, he said, "Wouldn't it be nice if this thing could do the garden?" The Golem began to revive.

"Do the garden, do the garden," he repeated. He rose and took the garden tools in the basement. Tillie was very happy. "We won't have to pay the gardener."

The Weightlifter

H. Charm
Grade 10

There once was a weightlifter
Who was stronger than all.
He was built like a house
And was seven feet tall.

With just one hand
He could lift over five hundred pounds
With ease, like it were a pinch of sand.
His arms were fifty inches round.

He could stop a car from taking a fall
That's how he got the nickname the Monstrous Wall.
His shoulders were at least four feet wide,
And, by looking at him, one could have died.

He looked like an enormous bull
That could ram you down to the ground.
He runs and moves as fast
As the fastest greyhound.

But, if you ever got to know this imposing man,
Who appears to be so mean,
You'd see that he's rather nice,
And his looks are not quite what they seem.

The Thief
David Taubman
Grade 10

Every night he would sneak into a house
Being as quiet as a mouse.
He would take everything in sight
And wouldn't even put up a fight.
He'd take the sugar; he'd take the honey;
He'd take the cake, and he'd take the money.
He would go to the 'fridge and take all the food;
His attitude was very crude.
He would steal the stuff of all these fools,
Take their credit cards and their jewels.
He would make a very big mess,
And then he'd get caught, and he would confess
Because he put the stuff up for sale,
Then the police would escort him to jail.

A Perfect Person
Yoni Garber
Grade 12

A perfect person, is there such a thing?
He would have to be humble, I suppose like a king.
With perfect fingers to move around
And not overweight, no, not one pound.
Perfect eyes to see and nose to smell,
And perfect hair, won't he look so swell.
When he talks, only words of truth come out,
In a soft sweet voice he does not shout.
But a perfect person is hard to find;
Everyone is different in his or her own kind.
A perfect person does not exist today,
But I can assure you everyone is perfect in his or her own way.

The Football Player
Dov Weinberger
Grade 10

He starts to train in the summer
In preparation for opening day.
He works very hard in practice
To be ready for his turn to play.

In order to qualify for his job,
One must be physically fit,
For his job requires an immense amount of strength
So that he can withstand and deliver the hit.

When game day comes
There is no doubt that he will be ready;
He spends hours studying film
And works out; he's been steady.

He plays with all of his might
Despite all the hits he's endured
And does his part on the field
In hope to have a win ensured.
At the end of the day
He must recuperate from the physical game
Then go out and begin to prepare
So his level of intensity next week will be the same.

This long and hard season will last seventeen weeks
In which he will give all and everything
And play very hard every week
All in hope of getting his Super Bowl ring.

Laziness
Eliot Orenstein
Grade 12

When I was a child everyone tried to instill the virtues of hard work in me. Since then, I have been intrigued by our negative perception of laziness. After all, society's successful have it easier in life; the unsuccessful have it harder. Work hard now so that you will have it easier later on. I realized that this old saw actually supports laziness.

People have a right to rest. Why should rest, which relaxes the mind and body, not be relished as much as work? If the lack of rest hinders productivity, abundant rest enhances it. Laziness fuels creativity. For example, when required to write a paper of a specified number of pages, bigger letters fill the pages faster. The elimination of contractions DOES NOT hurt either. Additionally, seeking to fulfill requirements while doing the least work necessary is not bad, it is efficient. Don't we admire efficiency?

Laziness leads to enlightenment as efficiently as eager effort. Hard work does the job for some, but for others a focus on the pleasing leads to the goal more swiftly. You might want to consider joining me in following the Path of Laziness, which is barely a path at all. The ideal is to settle into perfect laziness. Let the stiff-necked, pretzel-bodied, introspective labor-worshippers continue their rigorous self-torture. Channel your thoughts in the right direction. Do not let them prevent your enjoyment. Forget the guilt that keeps others working all day. Let that which really matters come without striving for it. This requires practice, as many have spent years continuously refining their methods. Following the Lazy Path is not easy.

The successful Laze must directly confront ascetics who attempt to project their self-discipline upon you, and reclaim the terms of value, which have been abused and slandered. Lazy is a good word. It is much better than *productive* or *assiduous*. *I'll do it later* is a good phrase. It puts things into their proper perspective. *Because I want to* is a good reason. Those who are non-believers will ask questions regarding philosophy, cosmology, psychology, etc. *Because I want to* satisfies the Laze.

Develop the right action for the moment. Practice particularly enjoyable activities in an attempt to infuse your life with pleasure. The right action will become obvious to you once you let go of your responsibilities. Drop that rigid schedule that was drilled into you by society and have a good time! The appropriate action? Laziness!

Perfect the art of exerting the minimal effort needed to achieve those goals that you wish to achieve. If this means no effort, so much the better! When you can swim through the month as through a warm pool on a cool summer afternoon then you know you are doing it right.

Rescued?

Michael Bernstein
Grade 9

For eight years, Jack Mellin had been alone. He only needed food, water, and a place to go to the bathroom, and he'd had all of those. Whenever he'd have free time, he'd practice his hunting with his spear. He'd gotten quite good at it, actually.

Finally, Jack was rescued, by accident. The Navy exploration ship had landed to escape a storm, and the crew had found Jack asleep under a rock ledge on the beach. The captain ordered him brought aboard. They gave him clothes and a bed. In the morning, Jack woke up and cried. Maybe he was happy, maybe he was scared, and maybe he was sad. We don't know.

The captain talked with Jack for over an hour, then emerged from his cabin, and addressed the crew: "We have an MIA on board, and we're taking him home. Thompson," he said, pointing to a nearby crewman. "Take us to base." Their base was in Hawaii, only 985 nautical miles from Jack's island. Why he hadn't been found until then, nobody knows.

Meanwhile, Jack was reading up on the last eight years. He was horrified to discover that there had been three bloody wars since he'd been missing. Three wars over (and this shocked him the most) nothing more than an election! He decided to take a nap.

The next day, he went into town. The people looked at him, some strangely, some plain scared! He realized he needed a shave. There didn't seem to be a barber in town, so he walked to a bus stop to go back to the Navy base. As he paid his fare with the $20.00 the captain had given him, he saw an old woman in the back, standing. He heard her ask a man who was sitting there if she could sit down, but the man gave her a disgusted look and ignored her, even though he had plenty of room. She asked another man, and he pushed her down, covering her screaming face with his coat. In a few seconds, the woman was dead. The man turned back to the window.

Jack was horrified. He stood, dazed, until he reached his stop. He knew what he had to do.

At the base, a ship was missing, a small, wooden, rickety ship, but seaworthy enough to sail 985 miles.

Jack Mellin was going home.

Sweet Julius

David Krup
Grade 11

Sweet Julius wonders why people steal
Sweet Julius wishes people wouldn't need to deal
Sweet Julius looks to find you a meal
Sweet Julius, hesitant to spin the wheel
Sweat Julius tries to keep an even keel
Sweet Julius walks left to right
Sweat Julius, at face value not much might
Sweet Julius, just because he doesn't really fight
Sweet Julius, it seems he can soar to such heights
Sweet Julius, the answers he gives are all right
Sweet Julius, it seems so simple
Sweet Julius, just like his good old boy dimple
Sweet Julius, he holds the door
Sweet Julius always has an extra dime
Sweet Julius, he sits with the poor
Sweat Julius can't even comprehend crime
Sweet Julius, kind of quiet
Sweet Julius would never riot
Sweet Julius, honest to his Dad and Mom
Sweet Julius does favors for his neighbor Tom
Sweet Julius helps his father
Sweet Julius, to him it's no bother

Where is Sweet Julius
Oh where have we gone

Descent

Zevy Hamburger
Grade 11

The scariest thing in the world is to have the feeling that you are falling. You have no control over what is going to happen or what will be your fate. The feeling of death is rushing through your head. Your whole life goes through your head, and you realize all of your mistakes and what you really wanted out of life. On your journey downward, you think, "Why am I here on this earth to begin with, and what did I accomplish and leave after me?" You get closer and closer to the ground, and all you can do is hope and pray that it's all a dream, but it's not. You're plummeting downward toward the ground; nothing is stopping you. 100ft. 50ft. 20ft. 10ft. and ....

Untitled
Avi Katz
Grade 12

A wise man once said, "To trust life in death's hands is nothing more than a wish for the end."

I must admit no wise man has said this, but I, a simple student of life, must confess the truth. To lie silent, to keep your mind dormant of all free will, this is to leave your life in the hands of death.

How you may ask? It's simple really. To analyze from all views is what can make us different from anyone else. Our point of view is the only thing that can change one's self. We all dress the same now and again and think like our peers. There is truly so much an effect they can have on our thought process to change what our heart and soul try to impose on us. Although this is true, we must not listen to those outer voices which are so loud but rather the voice from within. To ignore that is to put our own thread of life against a razor sharp blade waiting for it to split.

Revolution
Simon Papiashvilli
Grade 12

Come look at the sight.
Come look at the fight.

Cry out for changes.
Bash the leaders' faces.

Sticks and stones and broken bones;
Now blood will flow on the shores.

A new ruling class;
A new military mass,

A cycle of revolutions; so sad;
Wait for the white snow to turn red.

The Last Stand
Daniel Goldmintz
Grade 9

On a dusty plateau in a desert was a man named Abdul. He was sitting on a turret of a Soviet made T-72 tank. The sun was setting to the west leaving an orange-streaked sky. There were dozens of burning vehicles behind him. Abdul's tank was the only one which was not burned.

Abdul's dull blue eyes gazed into the desert, just staring, not focusing on anything. His uniform was torn and ripped, his faced covered in mud. His face also bore fresh battle scars. Abdul's face was a strange one. It was filled with a mixture of pain, sorrow, and anger. He clutched his AK-47 so tightly, one would think it was the only thing in the world he had left.

Abdul was an Iraqi who was part of a tank division which made its last stand against the American drive into his country. They had failed miserably. Operation Desert Storm had been a smashing success.

Beloved Mr. B
Yair Reuben
Grade10

There is a man very close to my heart,
    Not many things can pull us apart.
We have shared many good times together,
    Starting from the time I was as light as a feather!
Mr. B is a charitable and kind human being.
    When he talks to someone, he talks with compassion and feeling.
Here is a man experienced in all walks of life,
    When he reached age twenty-six, G-d blessed him with a
    beautiful wife.

He was born in Europe and survived Hitler's terror.
    When he came to America he adjusted through trial and error.
No person has ever had with him any arguments or quarrels.
    That's because of his high standard of values and morals.
A man of laughter and full of joy,
    He is the perfect role model for every girl and boy.
Anything I've ever asked from him was never a maybe.
    Yes, you've guessed it, he is my beloved Zaidy.

Title:?

Yosef Bronstein
Grade 10

A hush of excitement fell over the world. Man was about to leave Earth and live among the stars. The first ship of a full evacuation of Earth was about to take off. The last ten seconds were counted by all of Earth, and, similar to a magician creating an illusion, with a puff of smoke the ship was up in the air. As if in slow motion, the crowd assembled at the launch site and watched it slowly rise up in the air. Within a few seconds it was out of sight. People were still looking up to the sky far after it was gone, thinking of the future...

They were thinking of a future where man would no longer be bound to the Earth and would be free to roam the stars as he pleased. Where man would no longer have to worry about Earth's depleted resources, lack of ozone layer and unbalanced ecosystems. Humanity would have a fresh start on any of the empty and unpopulated paradise worlds in the universe. People would no longer have to live cramped up on the over-populated earth. There was plenty of room in the cosmos, and there was no reason why man should not take his share!

Those people were still looking at the sky when the ship reappeared, this time traveling back towards Earth. They watched dumbfounded as the ship landed back in the same spot from which it took off. It was as if the ship carrying all of man's hopes and dreams had never taken off. Slowly the main hatch opened, and all of the people in the ship walked out. With their heads bowed and tears streaming down their faces, they looked like they were on a funeral march as they walked through the amazed crowd, not responding to any of the questions directed at them. This was too much for the crowd so they blocked the procession and demanded answers from the people who were on the ship. As a response, the people from the ship all pointed to the main hatch from which they had walked out. Standing there in the threshold was a being totally encompassed in the black cloak it was wearing. No part of its skin could be seen, and it was, therefore, undeterminable if it was male or female, young or old. For a few seconds, it just stood there, as if waiting for a reaction from the assembled people and then, when the crowd remained silent, it began to speak. It spoke slowly and in the same loud, mournful voice a teacher uses when giving a child a punishment he really does not wish to give. This is what it said:

"People of the Earth, please listen to what I have to say. I have been sent here by the intergalactic community in regard to your recent plans to evacuate your native planet and settle on other worlds. You want to leave Earth because of the problems caused by its missing ozone layer, unbalanced ecosystems and lack of natural resources. These things led to widespread cancer epidemics, radical change of climate, and a dearth of energy and fuel that, in addition to the problem of overpopulation, made it difficult to remain on Earth. The evacuation of Earth seemed like the perfect solution and, indeed, from your point of view, it is.

"However, the intergalactic community takes offense at your treatment of your planet. They think of you as a disgusting race that exploits its planet as it sees fit. When the Earth is of no use anymore, you just move on, leaving a consumed and drained planet in your wake. What you fail to realize is that a planet is a living home that is to be loved and taken care of and not just a hunk of lifeless matter existing to serve you. Just like your small ecosystems on Earth become unbalanced even if just one component is missing, so too does a single damaged planet such as yours disturb the harmony of the entire universe. You are a destructive race and, if left alone to roam the galaxies, you would damage other planets as well and further disturb the balance of the universe. Therefore, the intergalactic community has decided not to let you go on with the evacuation plan and will quarantine you to Earth. You will have to reap the benefit of the work of your hands and live with what you did. However, there will be a way for you to break this quarantine and join us among the stars. You must heal the Earth from what you did to it. You have the technology to set up a new ozone layer and balance the ecosystems, and it is about time that you used it. Instead of running from your problems like cowards, you should face them and fix them. When this is done, we of the stars will know that you are to be trusted and will let up the quarantine. Until then, we will leave you to your own devices. Goodbye."

The being then disappeared. The reaction of the people of Earth was the same as that of the people from the ship. They broke down crying and did not stop for a very long time. What they had really known from the very beginning but had never admitted to themselves had just come out into the open. Man was shamed, disgraced and humbled before the intergalactic community. He was not about to fulfill a lifelong dream by evacuating Earth like he originally thought, but was about to commit a heinous crime and do damage to the entire universe. Maybe later when he was ready, man would join the intergalactic community; but as of yet, he was comparable to a trouble-making child who needs to be sent to his room to prevent him from doing more harm than he has already done. He must clean up his own room before going down to the main rooms of the house and join the adults there. It would take a while but, with time, even the most troublesome child can grow into a productive and upright adult.

Which Way Did He Go?
David Krup
Grade 11

It's that time, that time again.
Time to resolve, time to question.
They say I'm a "righty," but can I be left-handed?
I'm looking towards it. Is it the fire or the light?
I don't want to go astray, but maybe this is the way to stray?

Objective:
Mordechai Appel
Grade 10

Objective:	To attempt to convince a Jewish individual to join the Israeli Air Force, assuming, of course, he has 20/20 vision or better.

As far as aviation authorities around the world are concerned, the Israeli Air Force is the most highly trained and successful air force in the world. It was founded around the time that the state of Israel came into existence and has conducted some of the most brilliant and daring raids in air force history, such as the 1976 assault on Uganda's Entebbe Airport. Furthermore, the IAF boasts some of the most advanced fighter and transport aircrafts, as well as choppers, including AH-64 Apaches and state-of-the-art F-15 fighters. Also, in a simulated dogfight with U.S. Navy plans over the Negev, the IAF shot down the equivalent of 250 Naval planes without suffering one "casualty." In addition, the sincere dedication, motivation and determination of the IAF pilots is one of the pivotal factors in their air force's success. Thus, in essence, IAF brilliance is to this coming century what the United States Air Force was to a good chunk of last century.

Now in the 21st century, the IAF is placing more focus on recruitment then ever before. Although defending and protecting the state of Israel is still and will always be the primary concern, it is after all the pilots who make up the core of their air force. Now in the 21st century, the Israeli government is spending more money than ever on ensuring that their air force is prepared and ready to handle any situation that may arise. Now those critics who have always been saying Israel is a land "flowing with milk and honey" wish they could be heard saying "a land flowing with milk and money." Unfortunately it just isn't the case. Yet, as I have mentioned, the Israeli government channels a tremendous amount of their precious *shekalim* into their air force to ensure the success of their invaluable pilots. Consequently, Israeli aviators are highly valued individuals who are treated with the utmost respect. As a further incentive, most IAF pilots go on to join EL-AL international airlines and continue to fly into their late sixties, while some even continue on to high political positions in the Israeli government. The salaries and benefits of EL-AL pilots are pretty impressive, good enough to attract excellence.

As ironic as this may sound, the IAF is having recruitment difficulties due to the lack of an imminent threat of war. Over the years, many of the pilots in the Israeli Air Force have joined because of their eagerness to be portrayed as the elite, fearless protectors of the state. They enjoyed a low mortality rate, unerring marksmanship and an outstanding downed-pilot-rescue-team, ready to infiltrate enemy lines at a given notice. Furthermore, the pride and perfection of being a military aviator is something that no other position can match. While yesterday's pilots eagerly anticipated the billowing smoke of a downed enemy aircraft, today's pilots look forward to the faint smoke of their next cigarette. Yet, with Israel bailing out of Lebanon and the Pope and U.S. President actively pursuing peace, more and more IAF pilots may be finding themselves with their playing cards and rusting helmets. That, believe it or not, is exactly the point. Future IAF pilots must realize, as history blatantly dictates, that war is quite inevitable and that they will be needed sooner or later to protect the Jewish People. Prospective IAF pilots must further realize that when faithfully protecting their own country, they are joining scores of other pilots who have gone down in the history books as "true heroes." Thus, it is incumbent upon the next generation of IAF pilots to help retain their air force's image and maintain the motto "the few, the proud."

One may wonder why anybody should spend a good portion of his lifetime flying military aircraft for the land of Israel. In my eyes, the answer is this: When a Jewish individual first joins the ranks of the Israeli Air Force, he is not merely there to add MIG-21s to the side of his F-4 Phantom or to reap the benefits of years in service, but rather he is there for a far greater reason. He is there to protect the Jewish men, women and little children living in Israel's settlements and to ensure their safety at any moment. He is there to assist fellow Jews at all ends of the world and do whatever is humanly possible to ensure that they are not being "pushed around." He is there to aid in humanitarian rescue efforts in such places as Turkey and help put an end to ruthless terrorism. Now which job brings more personal satisfaction due to the realizations that you are helping thousands of people? What other job values your life to such an extent, that others' lives are endangered to ensure yours? And which other job allows you to work with the most advanced equipment in the world to guarantee the effectiveness of your efforts? These are the questions I ask you today. Take them seriously and join the IAF today, for who truly knows if you'll be involved in a dawn commando raid on some prison in Lebanon?

All in all, one must take into account that the possibility of joining one of the most advanced air forces in the world brings along with it something unattainable anywhere else. That is the ability to defend one's own homeland and country with honor, dignity, and those common features displayed by a true Israeli Air Force aviator.

Emotions
Shaul Lifshitz
Grade 11

Restrained
Imprisoned
Hungry
Sad
Happy
Tired
Mad
Crazy
Lazy
Hazy
Dazey
Nauseous
Glad
Calm
Excited
Nervous
Angry
Bored
Anxious
Free
Spaced
Awake
Cramped
Upset
Bad
Sleepy
Tense
Interested
Blank
Distracted
Achy
Stuffy
Cool
Are
All
Of
My
Emotions
When
I
Am
In
School

My Friend
Judah Rothstein
Grade 12

Today I lost a friend. I feel as if part of me is now lost. Although she is gone from my life, the footprints she has made will never be gone from my heart. They are deep footprints that have molded themselves into my being, into my soul. Today I lost a friend, and the very thought sends a chill throughout my body. True friends are diamonds precious but rare; false friends are like autumn leaves found everywhere. Today I lost a true friend, a true diamond; will I ever know what that means? The thought still sends chills down my spine and through my body. This friend has been a part of my life. She knows things about me no one else knows. Then I ask myself, why have I lost a friend? Why have I lost *this* friend?

I haven't lost this friend because I've done something wrong. We aren't now friends because she did something wrong. We aren't friends now because we have drifted apart, lost interest, or diverged from the same path. I knew that there was something wrong—we both did—but we both did nothing. It's amazing how one day I was able to wake up and realize that it was over, that our long friendship had disappeared. It felt like it had snuck up on me, like time had snuck up on me and then made the kill.

I've been friends with her for over seven years. It seems like a lifetime to me, almost half my lifetime in fact. We never saw each other much, even though she lived close by, but we talked on the phone a lot; she was always close in heart. She taught me to be real, to be true to myself, and to know where my loyalties lie in life. Oh, she taught me much more than that. She taught me about faith, about religion, about people, relationships, girls, even about marriage; I learned what I want to look for in a wife. It's a powerful feeling to think that I have changed a person, helped shape her into who she is today, and it's even more powerful, and even scarier, to think that she did the same for me. Part of who I am is because of her.

So, while she might be gone in presence, her memory, her being, now lives on in me. In all the ways I plan to make a difference, in all the deeds I do, some of the credit goes to her. This is true of all friends, of all people in our lives who help us become the people we are. Our friends, our teachers, our parents, and grandparents, even our enemies take part in helping us achieve a sense of "being."

Oh, I can find other people to tell my problem to—to share my worries, my dreams, my fears and hopes. I can even find people who will teach me about life and to whom I'll do the same; but, in so many ways, Devorah can never be replaced.

I write this down so that I will never forget her. I write this down as my tribute to her, and to our friendship. To acknowledge the ways she has helped me grow into the person I am. I owe you Devo. I don't know how the next few pages of our lives will look, if somehow our roads will pass or not.

A friend once told me that time was a predator that stalks us all our lives, it sneaks up on us in order to make the kill, in order to surprise us. But I rather believe time is a companion that travels along with us on the journey, reminds us to cherish every moment as it passes, for it will never come again. What we leave behind as we take the next step forward in life is not as important as how we have lived.

Why Would You Ever Smoke a Third Time?
Anonymous

If a donkey asked you if he could
poison you (a poison so potent that it
takes decades to clean it out of your
system, and that's if you quit)
and if a donkey asked you if he could
take your money, and
if a donkey asked you if he could paint
your teeth a hideous brown, and if that
same donkey asked if he could intertwine
its empty soul with the very threads that
protect you from the cold,
would you let him?

So, then why do you let a Camel?

Tasting Bitter Fate
Avi Katz
Grade 12

The cruel world, which I will know through all eternity, has passed sentence on my emotions again. To tempt fate is to wave a red towel in front of a bull. I have yet to disprove a simple fact. Our irony is G-d's humor.

I have opened up only to be closed down. The risk for which I question has jumped up and bit me. To not question one's motives is an invitation for pain, and no pain reliever is enough. No painkiller will stop the beats of this pain-filled heart. Whether that is good or bad I do not know, but I tell you this: loneliness has an advantage. I am weak and I do forgive only to get hurt again. If you have strength, resist that feeling for it will bring nothing but more heartache. To resist is to survive. You will find one day that this is a rule to live by and to never question.

Light at the End of the Tunnel
Shimon Rosenbaum
Grade 11

When you wake up you feel all alone,
You feel like you're not even known.
You go to school wishing those feelings will go away,
And you realize they're here to stay.
What you really want is some cheering
To get rid of all you're fearing.
You want to feel glad,
But it's hard because you just feel so sad.
You go home, go to sleep, and wake up the next day,
And you realize those feelings actually went away.
For people who know, an end seems never,
But, remember, these feelings don't last forever.

It Was Late and I Was Tired

Michael Bernstein
Grade 9

The circumstances worked out just right enough so that it was wrong for everybody.

There was a family whose name is lost to history—we'll call them the Shalt family. All one can really say about them is that they had a dog. It's sad, but in some cases that's all a family unit really amounts to.

But this dog was something else again. Its name was Peter, and its genetic code was the result of much experimentation amongst canine technicians and biophysicists.

Fundamental to Peter's DNA was a trait produced in a laboratory, the trait for loyalty bordering on zealousness. Peter had no choice but to be loyal to his owners, the Shalt family, once he had formed an emotional bond. For him, devotion to one's masters was as natural as breathing.

And so all was well. Peter never barked loudly, he never bit, and he was good with children of all ages. He was never found rooting through garbage or chasing cats. He was an exemplary dog. Everybody remarked on his good behavior, which was almost paranormal. Somebody joked that the dog's name should really be Saint Peter. Actually, several somebodies made this joke, which stopped being funny after a while, but the Shalt family bore it with good humor.

Nobody ever heard Peter complain, either.

The Shalts would gladly have let Peter sleep indoors, but he preferred to spend hours of the night outside. He managed to communicate this to the humans by dragging his bed through the back door every evening until they got the point.

Yes, Peter was a happy dog, and a happily owned one as well. But genes are tricky things. You can't defy the nature encoded into the particular double helix forming a daisy chain throughout your body. More sentient beings than Peter have tried and failed.

And one of the side effects of the loyalty gene—totally unforeseen for some reason—was a tendency to live the nocturnal life. Peter did spend an unusual amount of time sleeping, but the humans chalked it up to canine lethargy. What they didn't know, because Peter was always there in the mornings, was that their faithful little dog roamed the streets at night.

He did not make trouble.

He was a good dog.

And so it was that one night, in early July, Isaac Harlow was packing up a late-night barbecue when Peter wandered into his backyard.

Now, Isaac recognized opportunity when he saw it. His children had been clamoring for a dog for some time now, and this fine animal was apparently a stray. If Isaac had stopped to consider, he might have realized

Peter was just a little too well groomed to be a stray. But there was no tag.

This is sad, actually. The reason Peter wore no tag is typically stupid, and summarizes the answer to the question philosophers ask: "Why haven't humans dominated the solar system yet?"

Answer: Because we can't see past our own noses, and when we hit the moon that was just a result of some extremely lucky steering.

Anyway, Peter had no tag because it was assumed that such an intrinsically loyal dog as he should be able to find his way home without problem. This makes sense until you stop to think it through, which the Shalts never carried out. If they had, perhaps Peter wouldn't have met the terrible end he did.

All of this was lost on Isaac as he implored Peter to enter his house. Then, he brought down his children—the Harlow family had always been plagued with terrible insomnia—and the family enjoyed Peter's company for several hours until the sun rose and Isaac, a self-employed journalist, went to bed.

Of course they didn't call Peter by his rightful name. Instead, Isaac named the dog after his ex-wife's brother, George. (Isaac's poor taste in naming animals is, as you may have guessed, one of the reasons his wife divorced him. On the other hand, nobody could very well joke about Saint George unless the dog killed a dragon.)

George left at sunup and returned to the Shalt family, where he answered to Peter just as readily. He was loyal, but not all kinks had been ironed out in the genetic coding. Peter/George's devotion was now split between two families, Shalt and Harlow.

Oh, at first his affection for the Shalts outweighed his faithfulness to the Harlows ninety-nine to one. Then, after another night spent playing with the children of Isaac, his loyalty scales tipped a bit more. And by the end of August, Peter Shalt, also called George Harlow, was equally and fiercely loyal to both families.

Even this might have been all right if the two families had known each other, but this was not the case. The Harlows and the Shalts had never met, though occasionally would nod to each other out of politeness at the shopping center or what have you. The ambiguously loyal dog was their only link.

Not that Peter/George ever wavered in his complete fidelity toward either group. Though he was equally loyal, the extent and range of his loyalty was still tremendous. He did tricks for both the Harlow and Shalt children, he was well behaved during both noon and midnight walks, and he always, *always* came when called. Always. Peter or George, Shalt or Harlow, day or night, that never changed.

And then came the inevitable day…

Jeffrey Shalt was walking Peter. The walk passed uneventfully, with both man and dog enjoying the early fall sights and smells, until the two rounded a corner and came upon Isaac Harlow, who recognized his pet-by-night immediately.

"Here, George!" he cried, surprised to see George in the daytime.

Jeffrey frowned. Who was this man, and why was he calling Peter George? "Come, Peter," he said, glancing distrustfully at Isaac.

Isaac was puzzled. Who was Peter? And why was George with this man? It was obvious they were together, even *sans* leash (Peter/George did not have a leash for the same reason he had no tag). "C'mon, George," he replied.

Peter/George started to walk toward Isaac, then stopped and looked at Jeffrey. The expression on his face was that of a chronic nicotine addict and alcoholic being told he could pick only cigarettes or liquor, but not both. Or it would have been if said addict was then somehow turned into a dog.

"Peter!" called Jeffrey Shalt.

"George!" called Isaac Harlow.

"Peter!"

"George!"

"Peter!"

"George!"

Peter Shalt/George Harlow looked back and forth as his genes fought a submolecular civil war. His canine head darted from left to right. His ingrained loyalty gasped, started to speak, gave up and ran away screaming.

The dog exploded.

Nobody was quite sure what to tell the medical examiner.

Skiing in New Zealand

Zohar Kastner
Grade 10

Have you ever wondered what it would be like to ski in New Zealand? When one thinks of New Zealand he thinks of a kiwi, and yes he is right; kiwis are from New Zealand. However, that would be one of the minor details of New Zealand. New Zealand is a small country that has more sheep than people. The landscaping is one of the most amazing sites; it's full of mountains and snow, with peaks up to 12,000 feet high. Fortunately, I have been one of the lucky ones to be able to ski down these beautiful, tremendous breathtaking mountains.

It started on a cold August day. I arrived in Auckland, New Zealand and was already getting started riding the slopes. The next morning I woke up at five thirty and boarded the bus to Coronet peak, which is one the ski areas in New Zealand. I arrived there and got off the bus and looked up at the tremendous mountains. I put my skis on and jumped on the lift. It took about twenty-five minutes until I reached the top that was full of white pure snow. I started my descent.

With sharp turns and snow in my face, I thought I was flying like a bird. I wanted to stop to look at the view and it was miraculous. With mountain peaks and small rivers here and there, and kiwi birds flying in the air, I took one breath and continued down. I looked around and realized no one was there. The mountain was empty, except for the kiwi birds.

When I reached the bottom of the mountain, I looked back up and saw how big it was and said to myself, "Wow did I really do that?" One of my friends came to me and said, "Hey lets go do that," pointing to the mountain that I just got back from. I said, "Sure lets go." We rode up to the mountain and skied down, and I did it again and again.

This is not the only ski area in New Zealand; there are plenty more. Both beginners and experts can find a slope on one of the gorgeous mountains. Go to New Zealand — enjoy the pleasant weather and the unforgettable skiing.

An Adventure

Julius Strauss
Grade 12

Come and take an adventure with me
Through sea and air we'll go;
In a state of dreams we'll be
Come and I will show.

Behold the land that reason forgot
Behold a place free from thought;
How spectacular is this awesome spot
Where desires are not fought.

Look at the upside down tree
Or gaze at the blue sun;
Fly with the buzzing bee
Then over the water we'll run.

Sadly now our time grows short
And the day has long been shed;
With this, we should move into port
And I'll be off to bed!

Oh how awfully the night does hurt me
As it comes to take away my friend;
And I wish that this adventure would continue to be
And not come to an end

Time however has come to show
That this wish of mine cannot be done
And with this you have come to know
My wish is only to have fun.

Lucky Girl
David Krup
Grade 11

She comes from everywhere,
Here and there,
Buys high and sells low
Finds worms when looking for snakes.
She's a lucky girl, even when she doesn't know it, she's a lucky girl.
Doesn't know when to stay or where to go
Eats off her hand,
When they eat off the floor
If only she knew
She lives at night to sleep by day
       But still gets by.
Reads the paper, but from afar
She gets it even when she doesn't want it

She thinks she's sad but it's just a ruse around us
To be glad? To be sad? Here and there everyone is a lucky girl
If only we knew. If only we could step back and see…
But that will change
Now even we know
We are all "lucky girls."

Untitled
Jeffrey Kilstein
Grade 12

. Once upon a time, Joe Self, a young man who just entered college,
is rushed into the fraternity Gamma Alpha Beta, the most exclusive frat on
the whole campus. In order to obtain his acceptance into the frat, he must
complete the hazing process, to destroy a piece of property of someone that
he doesn't know. Pressured by his soon-to-be brethren, Joe takes a baseball
bat and, with a burst of pent up testosterone in his system, proceeds to hit
Mike Common's locker until it opens. It is at that point that Joe (to his infi-
nite delight) sees a wad of money lying on the top shelf of the locker. Joe
quickly looks around to see if the "coast is clear" (because it's only a crime
if you get caught). Upon seeing that he's in the clear, he takes the money,
sticks it into his pocket and, without a single thought to Mike, he leaves the
grounds. Though it is obvious that Joe was wrong, actions similar to this
take place every day; yet, when done, they are hardly considered damage.

People rarely think of the consequences of their actions in regard to those around them. Rather, they count themselves lucky if they do not get caught.

Attempting to rationalize actions by taking the unethical (and usually the easier and faster) way out, people say they're doing what others would do in their place. And, who knows, maybe they're right. Personally, I think free will is overrated. Hitler and Stalin used their influence to take away both the ability to think rationally and independently, and, at that time, their countries loved them for it. One just has to get past the fact that they were also called monsters and madmen and have the innocent blood of millions on their hands, but that's easy to forget, isn't it?

One could look at the Bible to see lessons of how we should act when faced with a dilemma of living ethically with a working conscience, i.e., the life of a civilized person, or to do whatever we want whenever we want, i.e., the life of a savage. Take a look at Moses: he was given a decision of whether to live a life pretending to be the Prince of Egypt or to give up his façade and let the Egyptians know of his Jewish heritage, thus losing his title and the easy life. Moses made the choice that marked him to be one of the greatest prophetic leaders of all time by being honest.

Take a look at our old friend Erik Hubbler. Erik is still working as an overworked, underpaid monkey trainer, yet his long-time commitment to his hairy primate friends has taken its toll on him, both physically and mentally. Over the years, Erik has become very similar to the orangutans with which he worked. He now has a considerable gut and, at times of anger, reverts to a primitive mode where he expresses his dislike through primal grunts and a display of scratching his rear. On one such occasion, Erik, upon attempting to back out of his parking spot, inadvertently hits a large expensive Lexus with the license plate "GOTTI #1" prominently displayed. After grunting and scratching, Erik realizes his quandary. As Erik sees it, he has two possible choices. One, he could look around him, see whether anyone had seen the damage done, and, if not, quietly and discreetly leave. Erik's thoughts suddenly leaped back to his dim days at Back College (a junior college in the heart of Hicksville, U.S.A.) where he heard of some guy Macaroni or Machievolli who once wrote that you should only care about yourself. "After all," Erik reasoned, "the guy drives a Lexus. If he could afford to buy such an expensive car, surely he could spare another couple of hundred to cover the damage. Besides, he should know better than to park here when there are idiots like me driving on the roads. In fact, it's his fault that my own Yugo got a couple of scratches on it; he should be thankful that I'm not making him pay for my damages!"

Then came the second option, the decision to take responsibility for his actions and leave a note under the windshield wiper stating his name, phone number, and what happened to the car. "In part, I guess I could be responsible for some of the damage," Erik thought nodding his head slowly, "I mean, I did have four beers at work."

Inside Erik's head the options are swirling around at such a pace that Erik doesn't even notice the suspicious looking man in a trench coat fiddling with the bottom of Erik's Yugo. Finally, with a burst of determination, Hubbler gets inside his car and is about to leave the scene of the accident when the enormity of this decision hits him like a heavy sack of legumes, much like those he would feed to the orangutans at the zoo. Is he ready to live his life in eternal fear that he would once again encounter GOTTI#1? Would he be able to gaze steadily into the bent bumper that would point at him like a crooked finger, forever knowing, penetrating, accusing? On the verge of madness, Erik realizes what must be done. Quickly he rips out a piece of paper and jots down the necessary information and places it under the windshield wiper. Feeling like a man reborn, he climbs back into his car and drives home, unaware of the bomb attached to the underside of his car, which dutifully blows up as soon as Erik reaches the speed of 55 mph, leaving his last conscience thought, "I guess I did the right thing after all...."

It is from Erik's example that one can see the correct morals to be found in a man. Though it is true that it was those same morals that blew him to smithereens so small that the police couldn't find enough teeth to establish a dental record, it is in any case irrelevant. By doing a good deed as his last action on Earth, some could say that Erik is, therefore, going straight to Heaven (though it is also true that, because Erik led a life of deceit and indecency, he is going straight to Hell. Yet that, too, is irrelevant to our point). Showing undoubtedly (or for the most part at least) that, by having the morals, one unlocks the door of deliverance to the soul permitting it to enter paradise.

Random Thoughts.....
Connected in a Way

Daniel Goldmintz
Grade 9

It is the
Little   things that makes one's day,
        not the
Big   things. In order to appreciate
        the little things, one must first have
Nothing—for such is human nature.

        It is the
Innocent   who try to escape, for that fate
        is not theirs. While the
Guilty   remain, for their   fate
        belongs to them. However
        the
Naive   neither remain, nor do
        they escape—for what
               do they know of   fate?

        It is the
Dead   who   cannot contribute.
The
Dying   try, but cannot either. However if
The
Healthy do not try to contribute,
           they are worse off than the dying,
           and are more dead then the dead.

How I Perceive My Role as a Jew in the Modern World

Chayim Goldberg
Grade 10

Being a Jew in today's world, I perceive my role as being both a follower and a representative of Hashem. While we worship Hashem, we, being his followers, represent him to the gentiles of the world. Having these two jobs, I have come to conclude that there are three characteristics and responsibilities that a Jew must have in current times.

The first characteristic is *middos,* or good manners. Middos are the definition of one's self. If you see someone for the first time who has no middos, your first thought of this person is what a bad person he is. On the contrary, if you saw someone for the first time who was helping others and behaving like a *mench*, your first thought would be what a virtuous person he was. As you can tell from these examples, a person's first impression of a stranger is based on his middos (or lack thereof). Because we are representatives of Hashem, it's essential that we be seen as a virtuous people.

The second characteristic is the obligation of learning Torah. Being the followers of Hashem, we must make sure our lives revolve around his holy Torah. We must make certain that it influences everything we do, for it is only possible to follow Hashem if we keep everything he has commanded us.

The third characteristic that I feel is needed to be a Jew in modern times is the responsibility of having a secular education. Although that in itself may not be equal in importance to Torah study, it is still important for one to learn general studies so that it may aid him in becoming a more intellectually well-rounded human being. Also, a thorough knowledge of the sciences helps one obtain a better understanding of the all-encompassing topics of the Torah. Even in historical times, figures such as the *ammora* Shmuel, or hundreds of years later, the Rambam, were both Torah scholars and masters in secular fields. Shmuel was a pioneering astronomer and one of the most famous of the ammoraim. The better-known Rambam wrote some of the most famous *Sefarim* on *Halacha* and Jewish ethics; yet at the height of his career, he was the head physician for the Egyptian Sultan. How can one come to say that everything but the Torah should be forsaken, while these great Tzadikim were major pioneers in both Torah *and* secular studies?

These three characteristics are the basic essential qualities I feel that one must have to be a Jew in modern times. In conclusion, it's my hope that all of us meet these qualities to live our lives as G-d fearing Jews and represent Him to the world in the best manner possible.

Pearls of Wisdom

The
Faculty of

The Marsha Stern Talmudical Academy
Yeshiva University High School for Boys

פנינה בינה

Imperfect Beauty

Sandra Schamroth

Your purple and red and yellow hues
Outline the masses of stone and glass and soot.
Jagged edges are softened; angry colors are lightened.
A dash of purity blinds the eager and littered streets.
From far away, its features seem unblemished.

To think your presence profits
From our neglect and greed:
The ultimate paradox.

Upgrading an Image
Dr. Arthur Hirshorn

The rat, along with the cockroach and the snake, is surely one of the world's most disliked animals. Down through the ages, rats have been held responsible for millions of human deaths. During the 13th and 14th centuries, more than 20 million Europeans succumbed to the "Black Death," or bubonic plague, which was spread throughout the continent by flea-infested rats.

The rat that city dwellers know and hate is known in scientific circles as *Rattus norvegicus*, or more commonly as the Norway rat. Other printable names it is known by are the brown rat, sewer rat, house rat, and wharf rat. Naturally, you would assume that its native land is Norway. Not true. In fact, the Norway rat is a native of the Orient, coming from the frigid plains of northern Asia. They were given the name "Norway" rat because many were spotted disembarking from Norwegian commercial vessels in the ports of Great Britain and the United States.

Norway rats are burrowing rodents, constructing their homes in subsurface areas. In rural environments, their underground shelters protect them from predators like the weasel and great horned owl. Moreover, their preference for living underground is not surprising when you consider that in Siberia and Mongolia (their ancestral homes), winter temperatures can dip to 60° below zero.

In New York City, they have retained their subterranean lifestyle to avoid detection by people rather than to escape the cold. They are commonly found in cellars, sewers, subway tunnels, and in underground burrows in public parks and vacant lots. Although there probably are as many Norway rats in New York City as people, they are rarely seen. Because of their inconspicuous gray-brown coat, silent and rapid movements, wariness, and nocturnal feeding habits, they are usually glimpsed as fleeting shadows at dawn and dusk. Early-morning and late-afternoon joggers in Central Park can attest to this fact.

Norway rats are similar in length and weight to their tree-dwelling city relative, the gray squirrel. However, their long, pointed faces and naked tails are quite distinctive. In addition, their hind legs are much longer and stronger than their forelegs. This characteristic makes them good jumpers and leapers as well as excellent swimmers. Longshoremen will testify to the aquatic skill of the wharf rat, especially its ability to swim underwater for up to three minutes.

In the city, food availability poses no problem for the rat. Like us, the rat is an omnivore, which means it can digest both vegetable and animal material. Further, when a food shortage occurs, they will even eat leather, glue and soap. Unfortunately, they also invade grain warehouses and silos, eating and spoiling millions of dollars worth of corn, wheat, and oats each year in the United States.

Another troublesome characteristic of the Norway rat is its extremely high rate of reproduction. Females become sexually mature at three to five months, and are capable of giving birth to as many as 100 offspring in a single year. Fortunately for New Yorkers, the lack of additional food and space prevents a rate "population explosion." In any case, the adaptable rat has evolved its own solution for this problem. When their numbers increase too rapidly, the adolescent females remain infertile. Their uterus becomes thin, and their ovaries cease functioning.

All rodents are gnawing animals. The Norway rat is no exception. With his strong, sharp incisor teeth (which grow continuously), the rat easily cracks hard foods, and can eat through wood, plaster, insulated wire, solid aluminum, and even concrete in constructing his living quarters.

Needless to say, many uncomplimentary things have been said about this particular rodent. Even the word "rat" by itself carries a negative connotation.

Who can forget James Cagney's immortal "You dirty rat!"? Then there is the description of a dirty, cluttered apartment as a "rat trap." When your pencil point or shoelace breaks, what do you exclaim? "Oh, rats!" And when a person betrays your confidence, they either "ratted" or "squealed" on you. The list goes on and on....

Even *Funk & Wagnall's Dictionary* defines rat (slang) as a "cowardly or selfish person who deserts or betrays his associates."

However, a more accurate description of the Norway rat would reveal it to be a very sociable mammal which, if anything, is much more adaptable than many of his rodent relatives, and perhaps a bit more intelligent.

Forlorn and One Hundred Years Ago

Dr. Geoffrey S. Cahn

Elliott Roosevelt's tragic life ended one hundred years ago today. Despite his failures and excessive lifestyle, which caused him and those closest to him irreparable harm, Elliott, who happened to be President Theodore Roosevelt's brother and First Lady Eleanor's father, was one of the most well-liked men in late Victorian New York and Long Island society. Considered by both friends and family members the "most loveable Roosevelt," Elliott was handsome and irresistibly charming; women found him extraordinarily appealing. Warm, generous, romantic, Elliott, however, could concentrate on little else but pleasure; unlike older brother Theodore, his life lacked a sense of direction and he was desperately incapable of achieving success through hard work. Ultimately driven to self-destruction by the responsibilities unmet, Elliott's story is forlorn yet moving.

His great sensitivity and benevolence was apparent at an early age. When he was seven, he went for a walk one cold morning wearing a brand new overcoat but returned without it. When asked what had happened, he explained that he had given his coat to an urchin who appeared cold. Taller, more handsome and convivial, and better coordinated than Theodore, Elliott's future initially seemed more promising. But the younger Roosevelt must have felt overwhelmed by his brother's utmost endeavors to excel in everything he did and realized that he could no longer compete with him. Elliott could not study with Theodore simply because he was not at the same level as his older brother. Though he claimed never to be envious of Theodore's achievements, Elliott never acknowledged the jealousy which raged inside of him.

Unable to live up to his father's expectations, Elliott's anxiety increased and at times became debilitating. By the age of fourteen, Elliott's apparent anxiety disorder had fully manifested itself in peculiar seizures, fainting spells, and fits of disorientation. For this reason, just at the time when it was decided that Theodore would go to college, Mr. Roosevelt concluded that Ellie could not pursue a future higher education. Packed off to boarding school at St. Paul's in Concord, New Hampshire, Elliott in the first few weeks did well, but soon was paralyzed by severe headaches which led to his withdrawal.

Convinced that Elliott's "physical" malady could be cured by strenuous outdoor activities, father sent him to the army post at Fort McKivett in the Texas hill country, where he would stay with one of Theodore Sr.'s old friends, an army officer. There his headaches disappeared as he completely immersed himself in activities like riding and hunting. It seemed that the further away Elliott was from his demanding father and responsibilities, the less prone he was to these infirmities. But this also meant the end of any organized program of study. The experiences gained there, however, made Elliott an expert in camping, hunting, fishing, and riding. Roused by Elliott's wonderful experiences of "roughin' it," brother Theodore would later emulate him.

Any tranquility gained by Elliott on the trip during 1876 and 1877 was shattered the following year by his father's sudden illness and subsequent death. Hardly leaving his father's room or taking time out to eat or sleep for weeks, Elliott's devotion to his dying parent was both heroic and exhausting. Throughout the rest of his life, Elliott was, according to sister Corinne, "haunted by his father's agonized cries for ether and the mercy of a chloroform sleep." "Nellie" (the feminine nickname Roosevelt, Sr. gave the weaker of his two sons in his dying moments) would never quite recover from his father's death. His inability to keep him alive must have contributed to the boy's already present feeling of ineptitude.

Deprived of the elder's guidance and discipline, this most sensitive of the Roosevelt children felt confused and lonely and began to drift through life as a sportsman, traveler, and man about town. Employed at Uncle James Gracie's bank in downtown New York, Elliott began to drink heavily and sought refuge on a trip west with Theodore. The two brothers seemed happy together, but their travels went askew when their rowboat overturned on a lake in Iowa, nearly drowning both of them. Though they shot some four hundred birds, the hunting was not as good as they expected. The whole experience paled in comparison with Elliott's earlier trip to Texas and upcoming hunting expeditions to India.

He was one of the first Americans to make such a trip. There he hunted tigers and elephants but also was a keen and sympathetic observer of the people there. Moved by the extensive poverty, he wrote, "How could beings created in the image of God be brought so low." He wanted to write a book based on his travel notes, and though he was a sound writer, he was unable to put it all together. Finally in 1933, some fifty years later, daughter Eleanor edited and published the manuscript along with his letters, under the title *Hunting Big Game in the Eighties*.

Elliott returned to New York triumphantly, an accomplished traveler. After India he also visited Ceylon, Singapore, Saigon, Honk Kong, and Canton. He was welcomed into upper New York society and vowed to make a fresh start. He joined the family real estate firm in downtown Broadway. He helped Theodore and others organize a local political reform club, and like other Roosevelts, representative of their class, volunteered his services to the Orthopedic Hospital, Newsboys' Lodging House, and Children's Aid Society. But like many in his social set, Elliott's penchant for drink was worsened by peer pressure from the racy Long Island crowd in which he and his newly-wed wife would now move.

The Roosevelt family hoped that Elliott's marriage to the tall and slender fair-haired belle Anna Rebecca Hall (b. 17 March 1863, New York City, d. 7 December 1892, New York City) would give him a new purpose in life. The New York dailies referred to the wedding on 1 December 1883 as "one of the most brilliant social events of the season." After the honeymoon, Elliott went to work for his wife's family's large real estate firm to supplement the $15,000 annual income he and Anna shared between them. Although the young couple was able to afford such luxuries as a well-staffed brownstone in the fashionable Thirties, Elliott clearly felt uncomfortable competing with the wealthier Astors and Vanderbilts, whom they mingled with. Ill-at-ease in the business world – "How I covet, yet how I hate the almighty dollar," he proclaimed – Elliott was unsuccessful at work and never able to fulfill what others expected of him. Burdened by self-doubt, he was further frustrated in his marriage to a woman who embodied perfection. Elliott felt increasingly unworthy.

Mother Roosevelt had remained the one anchor in his unstable life and her death in 1884 made him inconsolable. He once again began to drink heavily as his marriage deteriorated further. However, when Elliot's first child, Anna Eleanor, was born several months later, she appeared like "a miracle from heaven." The love between father and daughter was extraordinary. Eleanor never doubted that she stood first in his heart. Likewise father became the center of her world and, in her mind at least, provided her with the ideals she tried to emulate the rest of her life — nobility, courage, erudition, devotion, and kindness.

Nonetheless Elliott remained anxious and capricious and spent much time away from home at his club in Meadow Brook, Long Island, where he pursued the life of a sportsman. He had given up his position in the Ludlow firm and the time spent at Meadow Brook took such priority that he built a house nearby in Hempstead where he would become a daring polo player, steeplechase rider, and fox-hunter. Always trying to prove his valor to others and himself, he rode with abandon and broke his arm and collarbone in separate falls in fox chases in 1887.

One time, while practicing double somersaults for an amateur circus, he fractured his ankle. Badly set, the ankle had to be rebroken and reset and the foot had to be stretched daily to avert its shortening. In tremendous pain, Elliott turned to laudanum and morphine and once again began to drink heavily. He was elated by the birth of his first son, Elliott, in Autumn 1889, but his addiction to drugs and alcohol worsened and he spoke about suicide candidly. Doctors prescribed a complete rest cure, so without even saying good-bye to his family, he left for the South by the end of 1889.

Barely recovered, Elliott would return to his wife and two children the following year but would soon have a relapse. In an effort not to lose his family, he decided to go abroad with them to health spas. But Elliott would soon return to his old reckless ways, more erratic than ever. While in Paris, he left his family for days, taking up with a married American woman. When Theodore heard of the affair, he got so enraged that he called his brother "a maniac morally as well as mentally."

An even greater humiliation confronted the Roosevelt family upon their return to New York, when one of Elliott's former maids, Katy Mann, told TR that his brother had gotten her pregnant and demanded $10,000 for her silence. Elliott denied the accusation and TR decided to call her bluff. Katy claimed that she could provide a locket and love letters Elliott had given her. When the illegitimate child was born, Teddy secretly visited the mother and was stunned to see wrapped in Katy's arms a child with "distinctly Rooseveltian features — an unexpected nephew." Afraid that this scandal would damage his political career and the good family name, TR secretly paid Katy and decided to place his brother in an asylum outside of Paris.

However, when Anna and Bamie, along with TR, went to court to have Elliott declared legally insane and his property (valued at $175,000) placed in a family trust, the news leaked out and made the front page of all the New York dailies. In a formal reply printed in the *New York Herald* Elliott denied that he was either insane or an alcoholic and was "merely suffering from the effect upon his nervous system of too many riding mishaps." All this public exposure was more than embarrassing to the Roosevelt family, and so TR made an agreement with his brother that the petition would be withdrawn if at the end of his stay at the French asylum, he would undergo a five week cure for alcoholics in an Illinois sanitarium. He was not to return to his wife and children until he proved worthy of them.

For a while it seemed as though Elliott was making ammends and even took a position managing his brother-in-law's, Douglas Robinson's, huge timber and mineral holdings in southwest Virginia. He even became a well-respected and popular member of the nearby community of Abingdon, where he lived. Everyone was captivated by his splendid charm and magnanimity. He was especially cherished for his charity work in the impoverished coal-mining community nearby. For the first time in his life, he experienced a sense of vocational worth.

Elliott, however, missed his family dearly; a second son, Gracie Hall, had been born while the family was still together in Europe, and young Eleanor lived for her father's letters to his "Little Nell." Elliott's exile was further embittered by news of his wife's recent illness, especially since any attempt to visit the ailing Anna was denied by his protective mother-in-law and Anna herself. The next time Elliott saw his wife was at her funeral in December 1892, where he wept openly. Fearing that Elliott might now take custody of his children, Grandmother Hall quickly assumed guardianship in accordance with Anna's will. What a defeat this must have been for him, for now he would never have another opportunity to erase the anguish he had caused his wife nor be permanently reunited with his children.

Plagued with further hardships the following year — the panic of 1893 ruined many of his private investments and caused him to leave his managerial position at the Robinson estate; his son, Elliott, died in May of scarlet fever — a tormented Elliott once again turned to alcohol for comfort. The only remnant of his past which gave him true happiness were the few times spent alone with Eleanor — moments of intense joy for both of them.

Eleanor fantasized that one day they would have a life of their own together.

Elliott would live out the last year of his life under an assumed name apparently with two mistresses. He was drinking approximately a half dozen bottles of liquor every morning. One evening he was so intoxicated that he was unable to pay his cabman or tell him where he lived. Consequently, he spent the night in jail. In late July 1894 he drove his carriage into a lamppost and was thrown out injuring his head. Two weeks later, seized by an attack of delirium tremens, the confused Elliott tried to climb out of his upper-story window. Later, running frantically up and down stairs he stumbled, and with one final convulsive attack lost consciousness and died. He was thirty-four years old at the time.

Grandmother Hall decided that Eleanor and her brother should not go to the funeral. Elliott's death, therefore, never seemed real to Eleanor, and she continued to idolize her father, perhaps burying deep inside her feelings of disappointment and even abandonment. Theodore was overcome by grief and, according to Corinne, "cried like a little child for a long time." Later, he would console himself by having only pleasant memories of Elliott and would write to Corinne: "He is just the gallant generous, manly, loyal young man whom everyone loved."

In an unpublished short story Elliott's main character is a New York society woman who possesses "so many good and lovable qualities" but is destined for a tragic end. Later, when she contemplates suicide, she muses:

> My life has been a gamble. I have lived for pleasure
> only. I have never done anything I disliked when I could
> possibly avoid it ... I hoped against hope that something
> would turn up and pull me through.

Elliott's character, tragically, was not entirely fictional.

Convergence
Sandra Schamroth

They sit there
biting their pencils,
wracking their brains.
They think I don't understand—
that I don't have a collection
of pencils my incisors have pierced.

I was once in their seats,
scowling at my tests,
invigorated by success,
alienated by adolescence.

I always thought that it would be easier
on the other side of the desk—
no more homework; no more tests.

What they don't know is
that every day is a test
and they are my teachers.

The bell summons the beginning of the race
to disseminate information,
to make it apply to their lives,
to have it mean something.

And I embrace my daily tests,
become invigorated by success and
despondent by adolescents
who don't realize
I'm really experiencing it all
over again with them.

Head or Tails, They Can't Lose

Dr. Arthur Hirshorn

"Yook, Daddy, animals!" Jesseye, my nineteen-month-old daughter, was doing her best to alert me to several inch-long earthworms wriggling on the sidewalk in front of our house. The sight of baby earthworms on paved surfaces became commonplace this summer with the unusually heavy precipitation. Most people, however, excluding very young children and avid anglers, could care less.

What do you know about earthworms? Sure, they live in the soil and are a popular bait of anglers. That's a solid start. But are you aware that many forms of wildlife would starve without earthworms? Moreover, without the continual plowing of the soil by the earthworms, the roots of food crops would not receive the sufficient air and water.

An earthworm has a streamlined body made of about 100 ring-like structures, or segments. Each segment is equipped with short bristles. With these bristles earthworms slither rapidly through loose soil and mounds of fallen leaves. Their bristles also function as anchors. For example, when an early-morning bird or bait collector tries to dislodge an earthworm, the bristles automatically curve backward, securing the earthworm to its burrow. Usually, the feathered predator or aspiring angler ends up with about one-tenth of an earthworm. The other nine-tenths beats a hasty retreat.

A severed "head" or "tail" is a minor injury for an earthworm. These tube-like organisms can quickly regenerate a missing head or tail in the same way that a starfish grows back a missing arm or a king crab replaces a leg. Occasionally, a severed tail regenerates another tail. When this unfortunate genetic mistake occurs, both tails starve to death.

An earthworm moves sinuously through tiny openings in the soil. As the tail section elongates, the head contracts, moving it along like a Slinky toy. When the soil is compact, earthworms literally eat their way through. With each swallow, an earthworm moves forward.

Earthworms are heartless and eyeless little annelids. Despite these limitations, a series of five pumps sends blood throughout their bodies. And light-detecting structures on their heads prevent earthworms from exposing themselves to sunlight. In addition, an earthworm can exchange oxygen and carbon dioxide without lungs. Its slimy skin is its breathing organ.

Because respiration can occur only if an earthworm's skin is moist, it rarely surfaces on a hot summer day. Exposed to the direct rays of a July sun, an earthworm would suffocate in 15 minutes.

Another reason why earthworms stay underground during the day is to avoid their many predators, including most woodland and meadow birds, frogs, turtles, snakes, mice, moles, and raccoons—all inhabitants of New York City. In Australia, members of the Arunta tribe eat earthworms that grow as long as 11 feet.

Too much water is equally dangerous for an earthworm. Probably the greatest single cause of earthworm mortality is drowning. After a heavy downpour or several days of steady rain, the soil becomes waterlogged. When this occurs, earthworms must surface quickly or drown in their flooded burrows. Adult earthworms through experience "know" where the nearest supply of air is located and crawl rapidly under small boulders, mounds of leaf litter and fallen tree limbs. In contrast, some juvenile earthworms become disoriented and rise to the surface. That is why you might have seen small earthworms on the sidewalk after one of the heavy downpours during the summer.

True, not too many earthworms live out their entire lifespan of about three years. But to compensate for their extremely high mortality rate, they are reproductive marvels. Believe it or not, each earthworm has both a sperm- and an egg-producing organ. What does this mean? When a pair of earthworms mate, they both become pregnant. In short, each of them could be called "ma" and "pa."

In 1881, one year before his death, Charles Darwin had a book published on the natural history of earthworms. In it, Darwin bestowed lofty praise on these underrated creatures: "…it may be doubted if there are any other animals which have played such an important part in the history of the world as these lowly organized creatures." Darwin calculated that on an acre of fertile land, earthworms bring about 18 tons of subsurface soil to the surface in one year.

From mid-April through October, both young and old New Yorkers go fishing. Some of these anglers try to catch multi-colored sunfish from the shores of Van Cortlandt Lake in the rugged northwest Bronx. Others may cast their lines for catfish in Belvedere Lake in the heart of Central Park. But no matter where they go, on thing is certain: Each time one of them catches a fish, he or she will gain new respect for these Rodney Dangerfields of the underworld.

Johannes (9th Generation)
Dr. Geoffrey S. Cahn

According to Woodrow Wilson's emissary and confidant Colonel House, Kermit Roosevelt (b. 10 October 1889, Oyster Bay, Long Island and d. 4 June 1943, Alaska) was the brightest of Theodore Roosevelt's children and if he applied himself could also be the President of the United States. Unlike brother Ted, politics would never appeal to him; his romantic nature, however, responded to other paternal interests. With a keen ear for languages and a devotee of the "strenuous life," Kermit extended the family practice of the writer-sportsman established by Robert B. Roosevelt. At times, he could be the liveliest and most attractive of the Roosevelt children. His story-telling powers enchanted many. However, his mother described him as "the one with the black heart," and despite his accomplishments, he led an unfulfilled life that ended in tragedy.

In spite of his contemplative personality, the second son of Theodore and Edith enjoyed a more spectacular childhood than the rest of his siblings. Accompanying his father on a big game hunt in Africa and a treacherous journey through the Amazon, Kermit become an early advocate of the "strenuous life."

Considered the most difficult of the five children, Kermit was both willful and quite mischievous. One Fourth of July he could hardly be restrained from eating the firecrackers. He once convinced a dentist that his mother had hit him and had broken a tooth, leading the doctor to suspect child abuse.

By nature, the young boy seemed more like his mother than his father, though TR liked to believe that later they were "so much alike." Kermit, however, often preferred the quiet solitude of a shaded room to the brightness and noisy activity of the outdoors. "The dreaming eyes of wonder," which Edith referred to, concealed more than she imagined. At times, Kermit appeared detached and seemed only to care for his mother. Nonetheless, there was no escaping father's forceful sway for, according to Kermit, "Even as small children father held us responsible to the law of the jungle." At an early age, he was taught by his father how to use a gun. When he was eight, TR took him, Ted, and four cousins to the Great South Bay for a cruise, some fishing, and bird-shooting. By the time he was eighteen, Kermit returned from a shooting trip out West bringing back his own kill of prairie chicken, ducks, and venison.

Most of Kermit's childhood was spent in Oyster Bay until he attended Groton School, the traditional training ground for all latter-day Roosevelts. There he became coxswain of the crew team, played some football, and was especially proud of his endurance as a long-distance runner. After receiving some unsatisfactory grades, Kermit managed to do quite well — he stood third in his class in his junior year (after some stern encouragement from his father). He developed a great passion for literature and while only fifteen discovered the work of an obscure poet. Moved by the originality of a little-known book of poetry, *The Children of the Night*, he sent a copy to his father who (at Kermit's insistence) convinced Scribner's to publish it. Kermit, in fact, collaborated with TR in the review for *Outlook*, and so was largely responsible for Edwin Arlington Robinson's climb to fame.

Kermit did well at Harvard University where he developed fine writing skills and began to read the classics in the original. Though he had already learned French and German as a child, he eventually became fluent in a number of additional languages, among them, Spanish, Portuguese, Swahili, and Hindustani.

Before entering his second year at Harvard, Kermit accompanied his father on a major zoological specimen-collecting expedition through East Africa, which was sponsored by the Smithsonian Institution's National Museum of Natural History. Determined to put the man in the boy, TR gleefully wrote home, "the rather timid boy of four years ago has turned out a perfectly cool and daring fellow." In addition to becoming an excellent hunter — he killed seven cheetahs, which was a record unequalled by any other East African trip of the same duration — Kermit demonstrated tremendous courage on the safari. More than once he faced down a lion, leopard, and rhino charging him at full speed. As the expedition's quite excellent photographer, he risked the stampede of elephants in order to capture a close-up.

Though Kermit graduated from Harvard with his original class (he finished the 4 years in the equivalent of 2 1/2), additional journeys, including the ones in the Mexican and Arizona desert hunting mountain sheep, were pulling him away from any routine career. Having no penchant for the corporate world, he quit his first job as a manager of the Brazil Railroad Company and instead joined the Anglo-Brazilian Iron Company in the more rugged position of bridge construction supervisor. Late in 1913 he was given permission to join his father on an expedition into the Brazilian wilderness to trace the unchartered River of Doubt.

The harrowing exploration, which included many perilous moments, nearly cost both Kermit and father their lives. A leg injury which TR, sustained while trying to dislodge two canoes stranded on rocks, became infected. Growing weaker and fearing that he would become a burden to the already debilitated party, the former president urged Kermit to continue without him. Refusing to let his father die, he took over the leadership of the expedition and floated his suffering parent downstream under a fiery sun to eventual safety. Some two weeks later, Kermit almost drowned when his canoe was caught in a fierce whirlpool, flinging him and his boatman into another raging torrent. The native disappeared under the water and Kermit would have met the same fate had he not been able to grab a branch above him and drag himself to safety. It is clear that without

Kermit's devotion and courage, TR would not have survived.

Before leaving for South America, the young adventurer was court-ing his sister's close friend, the beautiful Belle Wyatt Willard, whose promi-nent southern family owned the historic Willard Hotel in Washington, D.C. Belle's father, Joseph, had been the lieutenant governor of Virginia and was soon to be appointed Ambassador to Spain. The wedding, which made the front page of the *New York Times*, took place in Spain after Kermit's return from Brazil. TR was very fond of his new daughter-in-law, but Edith seri-ously doubted that the blithe outgoing Belle could soothe her son's periods of depression.

The young couple settled in Buenos Aires, where Kermit became Assistant Manager of the newly opened branch of the National City Bank. Kermit freely admitted that he had no head for banking and that his chief asset was his congenial personality.

Kermit's brothers were soon preparing to fight in World War I and Kermit's quickest way into action was to secure a commission in the British Army which was fighting the Turks in Mesopotamia and Palestine. After being awarded the British Military Cross for his gallant efforts as Captain attached to the Motor Machine Guns, he was transferred in June 1918 to France, where he served in the First Division of the American Army as a field artillery captain commanding a battery of the famous French 75s. Always the adventurer, during the war he managed to visit the holy sites in Jerusalem and wrote ardently about exploring an island in Mesopotamia which he described as possibly being a "surviving fragment of the Garden of Eden." (These accounts were published a year later in his book *War in the Garden of Eden*.)

Having fulfilled his duty to his country and obligation as a Roosevelt, Kermit was at peace with himself for now and assumed that the world would forever be his oyster. The death of his father in 1919 proved to be a shattering experience for him. He admitted to his mother that "the bottom ha[d] dropped out" of his life. As much as he tried to follow his father's earlier direction, his inability to rebuild a stable life would eventu-ally destroy him.

The business he now chose would only partially satisfy his cravings for world travel. The shipping industry took Kermit to the Far East, the Philippines, and India. After forming the Roosevelt Steamship Company, which operated vessels owned and leased by the U.S. Shipping Board, the corporation eventually merged with the International Mercantile Marine Company, making Kermit Vice President of the parent concern. With pas-senger and freight trade falling off dramatically during the Depression, the shipping industry was failing and Kermit was forced to borrow money from Belle's family in order to keep his ships afloat.

Business pursuits alone could not satisfy Kermit's *Wanderlust*. His physical stamina as an explorer and hunter became legendary — natives on his expeditions demanded one day's rest for each day spent exploring at an incredible pace. Accompanying his brother on two major expeditions, Ted, an accomplished sportsman himself, would admit, "compared to Kermit I am a beginner." On the first such trek through Eastern Turkestan organized for the Chicago Field Museum in 1925, the Roosevelt brothers were able to bag 70 large animals of 20 different species and nearly 2,000 specimens of small mammals, birds, and reptiles. The most important catch of that epic journey was the legendary *Ovis poli*, a rare mountain sheep, conceded by sportsmen the world over to be one of the finest game trophies since it was considered to be nearly extinct. The second expedition for the Chicago Field Museum in 1928-29 took them into the Yunnan and Szechuan provinces of China. Among their collection of 40 large mammals, the rarest of game — the giant panda — was killed and brought back to the United States for the first time to be scientifically studied by zoologists and naturalists the world over. Back home, readers followed the Associated Press reports of these incredible journeys as if they were serialized fiction. The two consequential books, *East of the Sun and West of the Moon* (1926) and *Trailing the Giant Panda* (1929), which Kermit and Ted co-authored, are among the finest travel and wildlife books written at the time.

Like his father, Kermit was a serious hunter, but he was also a dedicated conservationist, much like TR and other sportsmen before him. As Secretary of the Boone and Crockett Club, of which his father was founder, Kermit participated in the negotiations with the Audubon Society to set up an antelope sanctuary in Nevada in 1928. The Audubon Society was so impressed with Kermit's diplomatic skills that it eventually offered him the presidency of the Society during 1935-37. He restored stature to the divisive institution which had fallen on troubled times during the Depression and became an influential spokesman for environmental and conservation issues concerning clean waterways and wildlife preservation.

As responsibilities of work and family grew — by 1925, his fourth child was born — Kermit eventually felt constrained by having less time for exploring, writing, and studying languages. He tried to distance himself from his wife's persistent social climbing. Though Kermit was amused at being regarded as a socialite — he often became the center of attention at high society parties — he didn't really like the type of life he was now leading. After a number of liaisons, in 1936 Kermit began a long-term relationship with a German masseuse named Carla Peters. Belle, who had constantly tried to save their marriage, attempted on numerous occasions to separate her husband from Peters. After urging FDR, who had become a good friend of Belle and her husband, to speak with Kermit, the President allegedly said: "Why can't you just keep your women on the side like the rest of us." Kermit not only ignored FDR's advice but later was forced to resign from his position of the shipping company he had helped found when his presence there became an embarrassment.

Kermit's life was spinning out of control. During prohibition, like many members of his class, he drank freely. By the late 1920s, friends noticed that he was getting drunk more frequently, and by the middle of the next decade, Kermit's heavy drinking and malaise were compounded by drugs he took to dull the pain of a partially amputated cancerous thumb. In the late Spring 1939 he returned to Sagamore Hill as a broken man from an unsuccessful alcoholism cure.

As the war clouds were gathering in Europe, Kermit strongly allied himself with FDR's more aggressive policies and wanted very much to be part of a military engagement which he felt was necessary. He also saw the international conflict in personal terms, viewing the war as one final bold opportunity to reassemble his past valiant life. In the Fall 1939 he met with Winston Churchill who secured him a commission as Major in the Middlesex Regiment of the British Army. In addition to participating in a special reconnaissance mission in Norway, he performed remarkable feats under fire, rescuing both men and equipment when the Germans later attacked in the Battle of Norvik. After the British were driven out by the Nazis, Kermit was transferred to Egypt but fell ill with malarial fever and dysentery and disconsolately returned home for treatment.

Kermit now began to drink even more heavily. Promising to check himself into a hospital, he suddenly disappeared, only to take up with Peters once again. Barely able to walk and a plain embarrassment to the family, brother Archie had him committed to a sanitarium in Hartford. Treatments there and in other hospitals were not totally successful, but Kermit apparently convinced the family that he was well enough to rejoin the war. FDR decided to give him the commission of Major in the U.S. Army with an intelligence post in Alaska, where he presumably would be out of harm's way.

Kermit participated in the September 1942 counteroffensive against the Japanese which consisted mainly of reconnaissance flights across the Aleutian Islands. Unable to take part in anything more gallant, Kermit began to drink again. Physical illnesses, which now included secondary anemia, forced him to undergo several treatments at Army hospitals in Vancouver and Washington State during the early months of 1943. He was eventually released, and after an extended trip with Peters, returned to active duty in Alaska. In a short time, he inevitably ended up hospitalized in Anchorage. Meanwhile, his comrades-in-arms destroyed the Japanese garrison on Attu, removing the last threat to mainland America. Realizing that he could no longer serve his country, unable to pull himself out of an alcoholic depression, Kermit shot himself in the head. Dead at the age of 53, he was buried like other fallen soldiers there, in a simple plot in the military cemetery at Fort Richardson.

Kermit had accomplished much in his lifetime. "Knowing him had been like knowing history," said Peters. But Kermit, the most sensitive of the Roosevelt children, had never fully recovered from the death of his dynamic father and felt that perhaps he had never fulfilled his father's expectations of him. The same indomitable spirit which drove Kermit and other Roosevelts to great heights, could also bring them to despair.

Mondes Éloignés
Sandra Schamroth

Are you eating dinner now?
What time is it anyway?
Do they have good food there?
What are you tasting? What are you thinking?

Are you sleeping now?
It's five o'clock here.
Do you have soft pillows and cotton sheets?
What are you thinking? What are you feeling?

As your day ends and mine continues,
Do you hear me in your dreams?
Listen:
Je t'aime

Acknowledgements

Special acknowledgement and thanks to the following individuals
who made this book possible:

2nd Avenue Delicatessen

Cooper Stuyvesant Cleaners

Mr. and Mrs. Josef Kastner

In honor of:

Shirley and Larry Goodman

Lotty Schamroth

Ruth Vine

In Loving Memory of:

Neil Benjamin Perkell

Leonard Schamroth

Doris Vine

Sydney Vine

ARROW FASTENER COMPANY, INC. ®

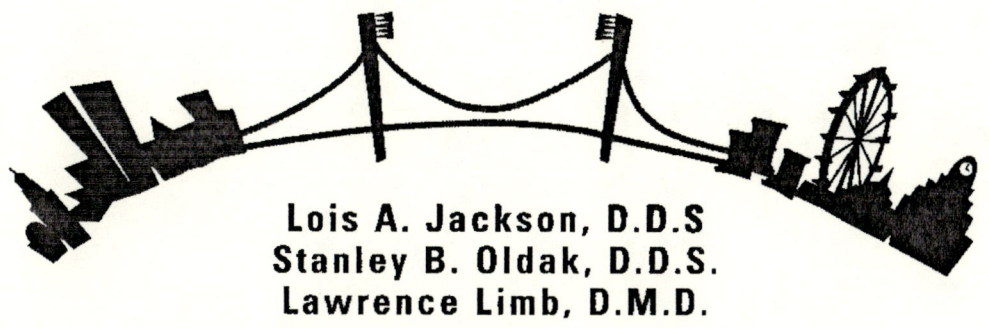

Lois A. Jackson, D.D.S
Stanley B. Oldak, D.D.S.
Lawrence Limb, D.M.D.

PEDIATRIC DENTISTRY

505 LaGuardia Place New York, New York 10012 212-995-8888
62 2nd Place Brooklyn, New York 11231 718-855-8833